NORTHERN LIGHTS
Lighthouses of Canada

Peggy's Point (Cove), N.S.

NORTHERN LIGHTS
Lighthouses of Canada

Written &
Photographed
by
David M. Baird

Copyright © 1999 Lynx Images Inc.
P.O. Box 5961, Station A
Toronto, Ontario, Canada M5W 1P4
Web Site: http://www.lynximages.com

Project producers: Barbara Chisholm, Russell Floren and Andrea Gutsche
Editor: Deborah Wise Harris
Graphic design and typesetting: Janice Carter, Lynx Images Inc.
Illustrator (diagrams): James Flaherty
1st Edition, August 1999

Front Cover image: Ferryland lighthouse, Newfoundland

Printed and bound in Canada by Transcontinental Printing Inc., Métrolitho Division

Canadian Cataloguing in Publication Data

Baird, David M. (David McCurdy), 1920-
   Northern Lights: Lighthouses of Canada

Includes bibliographical references and index.
ISBN 1-894073-09-6

1. Lighthouses—Canada—History. 2. Lighthouses—Canada—Pictorial works. 1. Title.

VK1026.B34 1999   387.1'55'0971   C99-931531-5

Apologia

In the last 25 years, Canada's lighthouses have been forever changed by automation. The days of lightkeepers tending lights and fog alarms, living in cozy red-roofed houses with nicely maintained grounds are all but gone. Indeed, only a few dozen stations in Newfoundland and British Columbia are still staffed in 1999, and many of those are slated for automation in the near future. Consequently, today at hundreds of sites across Canada, only lonely towers with perhaps a garage-sized service building stand. Such is the nature of progress and rapid change in a technological age.

My research trips to lighthouses span a period of more than 50 years. Many of the photographs in this volume were taken during the "heyday" of the lighthouses. The text describes the present (1999) condition with the knowledge that even that is liable to frequent change.

BC - 13

Triple Island, B.C.

BC - 15

Bonilla Island, B.C.

 Belle Isle South, Nfld.

Table of Contents

The old instruments of navigation, the compass (above) and the octant (right)

# Preface

The Canadian seaboard is dotted with intriguing lighthouses from Fort Amherst in St. John's, Newfoundland, to Pachena, on Vancouver Island. Ferries to Newfoundland, across the Bay of Fundy and to Vancouver Island carry hundreds of thousands of passengers past active lighthouses. Lighthouses are inspiring and romantic, standing guard in places that are often of unusual scenic beauty. They carry stories that run the whole range of human experience.

My own interest in lighthouses began at the age of 11, in the seaport of Saint John where I lived. I had the opportunity to visit Partridge Island light at the mouth of the harbour with my boyhood friend, the lightkeeper's son. All through my school years, the two-toned diaphone foghorn of that lighthouse station sounded through the frequent foggy nights. Years later, while doing geological mapping on the north coast of Newfoundland, I was camped for a couple of weeks beside the remote Change Island light station and got to know the keeper, his family and their daily round. Most impressionable for me was as a deckboy, receiving a mariner's view of the great Australian lights. I was hooked.

In the last few years, with rapid progress in navigation techniques and lighthouse technology, profound changes have come to light stations. A few still stand proudly on their islands or rocky points. The grounds and buildings are neatly kept, their keepers in watchful attendance, their fog horns sounding through the mists and rain clouds, and always, the beacon shines out over the water to guide mariners. Others are mere ruins with jumbled piles of broken stone and bits of twisted railings, empty foundations of houses, overgrown pathways, and stairs dangling on the edges of cliffs. Some even have small cemeteries with leaning stones and weathered fences that mark the resting places of keepers or their families, and dead sailors that washed up on these shores in storms. An old light tower may still stand nearby or just its foundation stump. The keepers' houses may have been torn down, with only a small shed filled with automatic controls: an array of solar panels; a radar-controlled fog detector; and computer-controlled electronic signals that pierce the grey fogs with their high pitched screams. But no matter what their current state, their histories are rich and filled with tales of relief and tragedy about those who sought safe harbour in rough seas.

My fascination with lighthouses is shared by many. Thousands of people belong to associations which focus on lighthouses, from history groups to collectors of lighthouse stamps to societies dedicated to the preservation and restoration of individual light stations. It is my hope that this book will contribute to the knowledge and appreciation of Canadian lights.

Pilot Point, B.C.

Introduction

Lighthouses have long captured our imaginations. They conjure up visions of solitude on picturesque headlands and remote islands. We fancy ourselves standing at the foot of soaring towers surveying the sea in its many moods. Perhaps we imagine seeing whales and seals, wheeling gulls and passing ships.

Actual visits to light stations occur mostly on fine days. We seldom see them in the noise and fury of gales when huge waves crash onto rocky shores and the air is filled with blown spume. We don't dwell on what it must be like to live at these lonely places through weeks of bad weather, with supply boats overdue, and no help nearby when accidents or illnesses happen. We can't imagine what it must have been like to feel our ship crash onto the rocks, watch the lifeboats snatched away by wild breakers; or to struggle ashore with no resources, waiting helplessly and miserably for rescue that may not come.

Canada has the world's longest coastline. To prevent marine disaster, thousands of lighthouses and aids to navigation have been erected. Some of them such as Peggy's Point, N.S. (Peggy's Cove) on its rounded granite cape, and Head Harbour, N.B. with its giant St. George's cross are common sights on post cards, calendars and tourist literature. For the keepers themselves, lighthouses provided a way of life most would not exchange for any other. Indeed, sons and daughters often followed in their parents' footsteps and, in a few places, several generations in turn staffed the same light.

Lighthouses are positioned to mark places of danger. It is not therefore surprising that most have accounts of nearby shipwrecks and tragedy. Along the coasts of Canada, the lore of lights is filled with bravery and hardship, ingenuity and endurance, tragedy and happiness in settings from wave-washed rocky islands to city harbours.

Why These Lights?

Canada has hundreds of lighthouses and aids to navigation. This book is a guide to over 140 of them, chosen for a variety of reasons. Some lighthouses have had prominent roles in Canadian history such as Sambro near Halifax and Race Rocks near Victoria. Very old lighthouses, still in service or well preserved after nearly two hundred years, include Isle Verte (Green Island) on the St. Lawrence River, and Trafalgar Point on Toronto Island. Great landfall lights, those first seen after long voyages, such as Cape Race and Belle Isle (South) in Newfoundland must be included, as are particularly remote ones such as Langara on the northwest corner of the Queen Charlotte Islands or Bird Rocks in the Gulf of St. Lawrence.

Some lighthouses are strikingly beautiful such as the graceful towers with flying buttresses at Caribou Island in Lake Superior and Estevan Point on the outside coast of Vancouver Island, or the tall, tapering lights at Cove Island in Lake Huron and Prim Point near Charlottetown. Shipwreck and tragedy caused significant lights to be built at St. Paul's Island off the tip of Cape Breton and at Pachena, B.C. Unusual structures are lights on caissons, such as at Prince's Shoal in the St. Lawrence, Southeast Shoals in Lake Erie, and the fortress-like Amphitrite Point light on the outside coast of Vancouver Island. Desolate wave-washed rocks draw attention to Triple Island off Prince Rupert, Red Rock in Georgian Bay and Gannet Rock in the Bay of Fundy.

Colourful daymarks, distinctive patterns painted on light towers to identify them, are unusual at Head Harbour, N.B., West Point, P.E.I., and Point Lepreau, N.B. Some lights have been selected because they are accessible to visitors and have become tourist icons such as those at Brockton Point (Vancouver), Peggy's Point near Halifax and Active Pass on the main ferry route to Victoria.

Cove Island, Ontario

The Beginnings of Lighthouses in Canada

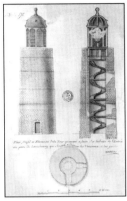
Louisbourg

The earliest documented lighthouse in Canada was built in 1734 at Louisbourg, the French fortress on Cape Breton Island. Since then, the site has been occupied by a succession of lighthouses. The reason for saying "documented" is the persistent rumour that the French had built some sort of beacon at Placentia, Newfoundland, some years before. The second light in Canada was lit in 1760 at Sambro Island, at the mouth of Halifax Harbour. It is by far the oldest Canadian lighthouse still in operation. Through the next half century, lights appeared sporadically but no systematic building program seemed to be in effect. A light was built at Cape Roseway, near Shelburne, N.S., in 1788. Green Island (Isle Verte) on the St. Lawrence and Brier Island, N.S., at the entry to the Bay of Fundy, were both lit in 1809 as was the Gibraltar Point lighthouse on Toronto Island. In this same half century, sea traffic, both commercial and naval, was increasing rapidly between Canada and Europe, and so were shipwrecks and loss of life.

Public pressure was mounting to build a system of lights to guard the principal shipping routes from Europe around Newfoundland into the St. Lawrence and along the coasts of Nova Scotia and the Bay of Fundy. The Great Lakes were also proving perilous in the last half of the 19th century. After the first surge of lighthouse building along these coasts at that time, a steady increase in marine traffic and the appearance of new ports supported a growth in lighthouse building. After World War II modern technological developments began to change lighthouse stations and the shipping that depended on them.

The coast of B.C. experienced the same history of increasing sea traffic, shipwreck and disaster with resulting pressure on governments to build light stations. The first lights came on line at Fisgard and Race Rocks in 1860 with others following in a steady procession, usually in the wake of marine disasters.

Pictou Bar, N.S.

Panmure, P.E.I.

PEI - 10

Cape North, N.S.

Red Islet, Quebec

Gannet Rock, N.B.

PEI-5

New London, P.E.I.

PEI-5

PEI-23

Summerside Range, P.E.I.

P.E.I-23

Caribou Island, Ontario

Gros Cap Crib, Ontario

NF-7

Cape Bonavista, Nfld.

Who Built & Ran the Lights

When Canada's first lighthouses were built in the 18th century, Canada was not yet a federation, and no central agency existed to coordinate lighthouse construction. Louisbourg light was built by French military authorities in the 1730s. Sambro, the oldest surviving lighthouse in Canada, was built by the Nova Scotia legislature in 1760 and paid for by a liquor tax, a lottery and later by fees extracted from shipping. By 1804 and 1805, organized commissions called Trinity Houses, following a British custom, were set up in Quebec City and Montreal to look after the St. Lawrence and its approaches. When Upper and Lower Canada joined together in 1840, a Board of Works was formed to administer aids to navigation.

In the Maritimes, individual commissions were responsible to their legislatures and in many cases joined together to finance major lights such as St. Paul's Island and some in Newfoundland, often with support from the British Admiralty. With Canadian Confederation in 1867, lighthouses were directed by the Ministry of Marine and Fisheries. The Ministry began a program of vigorous activity to upgrade existing lights and to build new ones where increasing marine traffic required them. Before joining confederation in 1871, British Columbia had its own lighthouse authority which built its stations, often with the direct assistance of the British Admiralty. By 1876, Canada's Department of Marine and Fisheries had established six regional agencies to manage, build and operate new lights along with hundreds of lesser aids such as spars, buoys and range lights that marked harbours along the thousands of coastal miles. In 1903, a special agency was set up in Prescott, Ontario as a central depot for supplies and expertise and to evaluate and research technical improvements.

A Lighthouse Board of cabinet ministers, members of Parliament and experts was created in the early 1900s to advise the Department and set policy. A government reorganization in 1936, reassigned lighthouses to a new Department of Transport. When Newfoundland joined Canada in 1949, responsibility for all aids to navigation on that long and difficult shoreline was also transferred to this department. Prior to that, responsibility had been complicated, being shared among local authorities, Britain and Canada.

In 1954, the newly organized Canadian Coast Guard took over and now has responsibility for lighthouses and aids to navigation through its Marine Navigation Services, in the Department of Fisheries and Oceans. It has fallen to the Coast Guard in the last few years to modernize the whole system with automation and destaffing, discontinuance of some stations, downward revision of some lighthouses to sector lights and the installation and management of marine traffic control stations. It is really a different lighthouse service as the century closes. Red ships of the Coast Guard fleet, and helicopters with crews of technical experts maintain the lonely, automated lights where keepers and families once lived and watched the sea and those that traveled thereon.

Southwest Point, Quebec

Construction Materials & Designs

Since the first stone lights were built at Louisbourg and Sambro N.S. more than 200 years ago, several distinctive Canadian styles have developed. Over the centuries, hundreds of lighthouses were built across Canada in a great variety of locations: from small, bare islands swept by wind and wave to tranquil clearings on wooded points. It was inevitable then, that a variety of materials — wood, brick masonry, stone masonry, concrete, cast iron and even fibreglass — would also be used to suit specific requirements.

Stone Towers

In Canada, the first light tower was built at Louisbourg, Nova Scotia, in 1734. It was a wooden topped, masonry tower, which was destroyed in 1736 when the open fire in the lamphouse ignited the structure. Its successor, made of local stone, was pulverized by British artillery in 1758. Canada's second lighthouse was built of stone on Sambro Island, at the entrance to Halifax Harbour and lit in 1760. Though modified from time to time, it still stands in service.

In many places, the same rocky shores that posed dangers to shipping also supplied the stone used to build light towers. The best examples are the limestone beds around the Canadian part of Lake Huron which supplied the flat blocks used in the six beautiful "Imperial" towers (erected 1857-60), including Cove Island and Nottawasaga Island. Local quarries were opened up and the stone transported short distances to the sites.

Imported stone was used at Race Rocks near Victoria, having been cut, dressed, and carefully numbered in Scotland and carried around Cape Horn as ballast in sailing vessels in 1859. The fine-grained limestone that makes the very smooth walls of the fat cylindrical lighthouse on Red Islet in the St. Lawrence River is reputed to have crossed the Atlantic from Scotland in the same way in 1848.

Granite blocks were cut from the bedrock just below the light at Rose Blanche, Nfld., in 1873 and stone for its recent restoration was cut from a nearby quarry. Local rubble rock was often used between brick or masonry walls. In some places, towers were built of wood and other materials on massive stone foundations such as at Gannet Rock, N.B.

Red Islet, Quebec

Point Clark, Ontario

Rose Blanche, Nfld. NF-14

Wooden Towers

By Canadian Confederation in 1867, wood had become the most common lighthouse material as it could be supplied inexpensively from nearby woods and mills. In some of the classic towers such as Seal Island, N.S. and East Point, P.E.I., timbers were hewn by hand and, after a 150 years, are still serving well.

Styles and patterns of Canadian wooden lights are quite diverse. Major wooden light towers as tall as 25m (82 ft.) mark prominent coastal features. The most common styles are tapering wooden towers 4-20m (15-65 ft.) high with metal and glass lamphousings on top. The smallest towers which graced hundreds of harbours, rivers, and back channels earned the sobriquet "pepper shaker lights" from their square shapes and sloping sides.

In cross section, the towers are square, hexagonal, octagonal or even round. Many of the early lights were housed in square wooden

Panmure Island, P.E.I. PEI-10

buildings with the light itself protruding from the centre of the peaked roof. Cape Bonavista and Cape Spear, both in Newfoundland and among the oldest in Canada are of this type. (Both are preserved as Historic Sites in their original configurations.) In the early days, keepers quarters were often attached to the towers.

Brick Towers

BC-12

Fisgard, B.C.

Bricks were imported in the early days and used both as linings and as the main fabric. Several brick towers were built but most have been hidden under coatings and coverings put on to protect the masonry from weathering. One of the most beautiful of all Canadian lighthouse towers is at Prim Point, near Charlottown, P.E.I. It was built as a tapering cylinder of brick, sheathed in wood, then shingled. The lighthouse at Fisgard, B.C. is made of imported brick, but was coated in cement and painted. The brickwork can only be seen inside, and on a decorative collar just below the light platform. The rubble heap marking the old tower at East Point on Anticosti is full of yellow, imported firebricks.

Cast Iron Towers

Cape Pine, Nfld. NF-13

Round, cast iron towers were built in many locations in the early days, particularly in Newfoundland and Nova Scotia. The plates were cast in Britain, brought to the nearest practical site, hauled to the prepared foundations and bolted together. In the perpetual fogs, rains and cold of the East Coast, cast iron towers and their keepers were plagued with condensation and hoar frost but were favoured because they were easy to erect and had low maintenance costs. In 1979, the Cape North lighthouse, erected in 1908 to replace the original wooden one, was taken apart, plate by plate, and, after complete restoration, was reassembled on the grounds of the National Museum of Science and Technology in Ottawa (see p.97). Cape Pine lighthouse, now a designated Historic Site on the southern tip of Newfoundland, is another of the major cast iron towers still in action.

Concrete Towers & Caissons

Father Point, Quebec

Caissons, set directly on subsurface sandbars are found at several places in Canada. A hollow cylinder was built and towed out to the site over a sand bar or mud bank and filled with water to sink it to the bottom. Sediments were scoured out to allow the cylinder to settle more deeply. Then it was filled with rock and concrete and a platform and light were installed on top. In some places, a foundation was prepared underwater and the caisson lowered onto it. (Note narrow waist design to avoid damage from drifting ice.) Notable caisson lights are those at Prince's Shoal and White Island Reef in the St. Lawrence Estuary.

Cylindrical concrete towers about a hundred feet high with flying buttresses make very beautiful towers at the famous old pilot station at Father Point, Quebec (Point au Père), on the outside shore of Vancouver Island at Estevan Point, and at Caribou Island in the middle of Lake Superior. A slender, reinforced-concrete column holds the replacement light at Discovery Island, B.C. Squat concrete or masonry platforms with only a lamphouse on top are found in a few places where height above the sea is not important or on cliffs that are already high enough to be seen far out to sea.

Prince Shoal, Quebec

Steel Stilts and Towers

Steel tower, Hope Island, Ontario

Structural steel legs have been used in a variety of circumstances to support the mounting of a small lighthouse on top. Slender, structural steel towers similar to radio transmission towers now hold powerful searchlight-style lamps, that operate in place of, and often right beside the old wooden and concrete towers. Father Point (Pointe au Père) Quebec, for example, has an automated tower right beside the old buttressed, concrete tower.

Range Lights, Bells & Buoys

Buoys, Parry Sound, Ontario

Range lights on shore stand in couples so that an incoming vessel can stay confidently in the boating channel by lining up the two of them. Buoys bob at anchor, shifting a little as tides ebb and flow. Some flash, others have large bells and clang out their messages as they rock back and forth in the waves. Still others carry strange arrays of radar reflectors, or bear the names of the dangerous shoals or rocks they are marking. All are carefully positioned to serve the mariner.

Stairways and Ladders

Cast-iron spiral stairways were imported for some stations and can still be found at Cape Pine, Newfoundland, and Fisgard, B.C. At other stations, wooden stairways lead up from the bottom level to successive landings 5-6m (16-20 ft.) apart all the way to the light platform. The stairways of some concrete towers are also made of concrete, as at Cape Race.

Daymarks

Canadian light towers are basically white, while the light platforms, lamphouses and their domes are painted a distinctive bright red, along with the roofs of adjacent staff houses, engine and fog houses. Early on, it became evident that when a ship emerged from the fog or in the light of dawn, plain, identical, white towers were hard to see against the snow or a fogbank or even an overcast sky. In 1860, one of the first duties at the new Race Rocks station was to paint broad black bands on the white tower to make it more visible. These "daymark" patterns also serve to distinguish a particular light from others along the same coast.

Cape North, N.S.

Gannet Rock, N.B.

NB-6

Southeast Shoal, Ontario

Victoria Range, P.E.I.

P.EI - 22

Point Lepreau, N.B.

NB -15

N.B-1

Partridge Island, N.B.

West Point, P.E.I.

PEI - 9

NB-3

Head Harbour, N.B.

Lamphouses and Windows

The housings for the lamps, the reflectors and lenses, and the lights themselves were mostly brought from Europe, the principal suppliers being Chance Brothers, near Birmingham, England, and Barbier, Rénard et Turenne of Paris, France. Their name plates can still be found in many lighthouses. Their round or octagonal lamphouses with rivetted copper or iron domes matched the designs of the towers themselves. A few had added fillips such as the tiny lion heads under the rim of the dome on Cove Island light. Unappealing aluminum lamphouses were placed on many old towers in the modernization period of the 1960s through the 1980s.

In very simple lights, the panes of glass around the lamphouse are plain squares or rectangles of window glass. It is characteristic of larger lights to have heavy, plate glass squares and rectangles or curved panes. The most elegant are those with triangular or diamond panes, set in metal frames. These are not common in Canadian lights but may be seen at Long Point (Twillingate), and Ferryland, both very windy spots in Newfoundland where extra strength is needed. Square frames in standard lamphouses also have minor blind spots that are avoided by the use of such patterns.

At the Coast Guard's Victoria Agency, the lamphouse from the ill-fated Triangle Island station is visible from the street, enclosing the large, original lens from Estevan. At the Parry Sound Agency on Georgian Bay, the gatehouse is topped by the old lamphouse from the Providence Bay light station.

Ferryland, Nfld.

Twillingate, Nfld.

Triangle Island lamphouse at Victoria Agency, B.C.

Seal Island lens on display at Barrington, N.S.

The Lights

Light Sources

The lighthouse story spans more than three thousand years, from bonfires lit on headlands or on small stone towers to automated, high intensity, revolving lights on skeletal steel towers. With bonfires, less than 1% of the light reached the sailor's eye at sea. Candles and batteries of candles produced better lights but were still fairly dim. Glass enclosures for the flame and for the lamproom as a whole, improved the brightness. Wick lamps were still better and burned all sorts of oils—whale, seal, fish, colzil and other vegetable oils—but their flames were still not brilliant and their wicks needed constant trimming. The smoke they produced also meant that their glass chimneys needed constant cleaning.

When Dr. Abraham Gesner of Nova Scotia invented a way to extract kerosene from coal in 1846 he discovered a fuel for lamps that greatly improved lights all over the world. Aimé Argand invented a system of concentric wicks with tall chimneys that made the light source far brighter. The next leap forward came with the development of mantles, lit by hot vapours produced by the lamps themselves. Campers who use Coleman lamps are familiar with the intense white light produced in this way.

In the 1850s, electricity made an experimental appearance on the world lighthouse scene with a brilliant arc light at South Foreland on the south coast of England. It was found to be too expensive to generate and maintain. When practical incandescent bulbs came along in the early 1900s, lighthouse lamps were modernized, and have since evolved to the intense lights that are produced today from mercury vapour, Xenon and other light generating gases.

In Canada, lighthouse electrification began in 1895 at Reed Point, N.B. and gradually spread through the system. The process was virtually complete by the late 1950s when the last few oil lamps were replaced. Acetylene flames have been used in remote locations and on isolated buoys since the Swedish engineer Gustav Dalen discovered how to use that gas at the turn of the twentieth century, and a little later how to have it switch itself on and off with daylight sensitive controls. This made possible the first automatic light beacons (for which Dalen was awarded the Nobel prize in 1912.) They were installed as early as 1910 in many remote places from the Baltic to the Straits of Magellan. A few automatic, acetylene lights still sit on remote rocks and channels and in the Canadian high Arctic. At many unstaffed stations today, powerful searchlights beam their signals from atop slender, steel towers.

Intensifying the Beam – Reflectors and Lenses

Reflector and lamp – Cape Bonavista, Nfld. NF-7

As the bare flames, used until the mid-18th century, were not effective enough in sending the light out to sea, reflectors and lenses were developed to concentrate light from the lamp into beams to increase their strength and range. William Hutchinson, a Liverpool harbour official, casually precipitated this revolution in lights by placing a dish lined with reflecting mirrors behind the flame. This invention quickly developed into parabolic reflectors of polished metal, making the lights many times brighter.

Some reflector-equipped lights are still in use at East Point, P.E.I. and Red Islet, Quebec, and several are preserved as historical pieces, for example at Cape Bonavista. This reflecting system was called the "catoptric" system.

Tinkering with glass lenses and reflectors began in England and France in the early 1800s. It led to a brilliant invention by August Fresnel of France in 1828. He placed a concentrating lens in the centre of his apparatus and concentric rings of carefully cut and polished glass around it. The rings concentrated the light radiating in all directions into the forward beam.

Barbier, Rénard et Turenne of Paris quickly became the principal suppliers of Fresnel lenses all over the world. Chance Brothers of England appeared on the scene in 1845, sharing the market with their own modifications and improvements. By 1900, marvelous lens systems were available to capture and direct virtually all the light produced from the lamp. They were available in a range of sizes, from very small to the enormous hyperradials, like the one still beaming from Cape Race, Newfoundland.

Simple lens systems were known as "dioptric" but when Chance Brothers and other inventors added multiple prisms to the central lenses, the whole became known as "catadioptric."

The intricate, polished glass and sculpted lenses of the larger lights are beautiful industrial creations. Most of them have been removed from

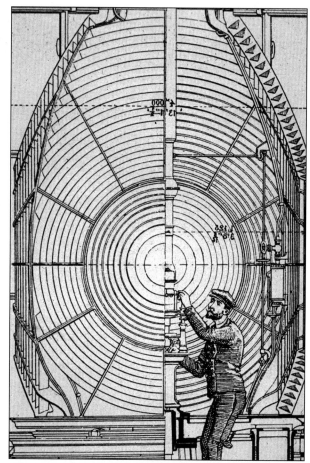

Chance Brothers Hyperradial

the stations, but several are on display in museums. At Pachena, B.C., the original lens system is

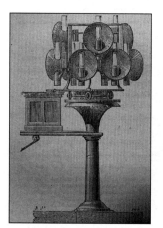

Multiple reflectors

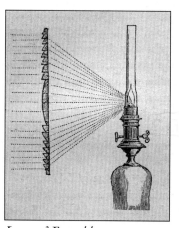

Lamp & Fresnel lens

4th to 7th order dioptric lenses

being kept in operation as part of the preservation of that wonderful, classical, wooden tower. The original glass lenses are still rotating at Cove Island and the greatest lens system of all is still in action at Cape Race. The Seal Island lens and its lamphouse are on display beside the main highway at Barrington, N.S. in a structure that resembles a smaller version of the original tower. The lens from Sambro is in the Nova Scotia Museum in Halifax.

Servicing the light, Point Atkinson, B.C.

Winks and Flashes

East Point, P.E.I.

When beacons were first built in a systematic way, lights were fixed and steady. They became dimmer or brighter only as wicks needed trimming or as globes became smoky and were cleaned. While they warned navigators to keep clear, the beacons gave no hint of their specific identities. By 1780, lighthouse engineers set about devising characteristics by which the light itself could supply a quick and sure visual identification. They began experiments with winks and flashes, working to develop a code for each light. Many variations and methods were tried but they all came down to three main light types: fixed, flashing, and interrupted.

Fixed lights had a continuous, steady light. Some of these had large lenses or mirrors to concentrate the beam in one direction and others were omnidirectional (see p.48).

To produce flashing lights in the days of oil lamps it was necessary to rotate the whole light and mirror systems as in the old Cape Bonavista light with its multiple lamps and reflectors all turning in one large unit. By rotating mirrors or lenses around a central, stationary lamp, flashes occurred as each mirror or lens came into direct line. With the invention of acetylene lamps and later electric lights, flashes could be produced by suddenly increasing and decreasing lamp intensity.

Interrupted or occulting lights were made when a steady light was totally eclipsed or blacked out at regular intervals by a rotating ring with one or more blinds. Coloured glass panes were sometimes used to give still another set of variations for identification.

Going Round and Round

The principle of rotating lights was devised in Sweden in 1781 and was soon adopted all over the world. By 1800, the light actually rotated by a clockwork and gear mechanism, which was wound up by the keeper. In the Cape Race lighthouse, the clockwork and its crank are still there below the great lens. Weights still hang in a square, wooden shaft, through which they traveled up and down every three hours. Lighthouse lore has it that some authorities preferred clockworks that required more frequent winding, thus ensuring the keeper was on his toes and on duty, day and night.

Mercury Float

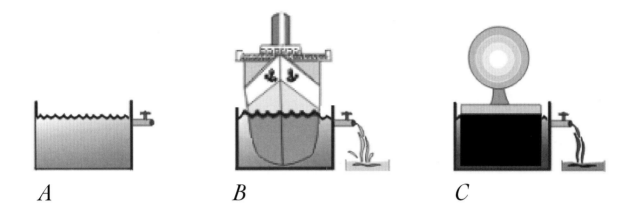

*A) dock filled with water, B) ship suspended in dock displaces its own weight in water, excess water drains out,
C) mercury float using the same principle – light apparatus suspended in liquid mercury displaces its own weight*

When the lamps and lenses had grown to several tons of glass and metal, the rollers supporting them were difficult to rotate. So, around the turn of the century, the lights themselves were floated in a channel filled with mercury. The invention of the "mercury float" was a major development, as it greatly reduced the friction and mechanical wear, and improved the speed of revolution. Weighing about seven tonnes, the Cape Race light is by far the largest in Canada yet it still rotates on 410 kgs (900 lbs.) of mercury. How does this work?

The first principle at work is that of displacement. A floating body displaces its own weight in water. This can be extended to include any liquid. The float in a car's gas tank displaces its own weight of gasoline to signal the level of fuel remaining.

The second principle is that the size of the body of liquid need only be big enough to accommodate the floating body. A ship on the open ocean displaces its own weight of sea water. It also displaces exactly the same weight of sea water when entering a flooded drydock, where the fit is close and the amount of water considerably less.

The third principle concerns the density of the liquid in which an object floats. Ships, for example, sink a little lower into the water when they pass from the salty Atlantic Ocean into the lighter, fresh water of the Great Lakes. The ship weighs the same, but to displace its own weight, it must displace a bigger volume of the lighter, fresh water. This was the principal reason why the inventors chose mercury: it was the densest liquid they could find to float the lighthouse equipment. Mercury has other advantages too: unlike other liquids, it does not evaporate quickly or thicken with age.

Some Canadian lights still turn on mercury, although fear of the liquid has led the Coast Guard to remove it in most locations. (To the writer's knowledge, no substantiated cases of mercury poisoning in lighthouses have ever been reported.)

Divergence

"Divergence" refers to the width of the beam emanating from the mirror or lens system. How long a flash lasts in the mariner's eye depends partly on the speed of the rotation and partly on the width of the beam. If the flash in the eye is too short, it will be difficult to pinpoint and to measure, so the divergence is important.

In the days of oil lamps it was necessary to use multiple wicks to get more light, and the beams got wider and weaker with a decrease in power and range. With the invention of incandescent mantle lights, giving many times as much light from a much smaller source, it became possible to make the beams much narrower and consequently brighter with much less divergence. Electric lights created even narrower and more powerful beams. Designers of lens systems allowed for this.

At Cape Race the speed of rotation and the width of the beam are designed to give four flashes, each of which lasts for exactly 0.3 seconds, as the massive light with its four huge lenses turns once every 30 seconds. If one is at a distance of ten miles from the light and the beam does a complete rotation in 30 seconds, the beams of light would sweep past at 3,800 miles an hour, three times the speed of sound. To be in the observer's eye for three tenths of a second the beam would have to be 1,580 feet wide, so the divergence has to be very carefully calculated, the lenses and prisms ground and mounted with great precision.

If one is near the base of a lighthouse, the lightbeam seems dim as it passes overhead and out to sea. That is because the downward divergence is

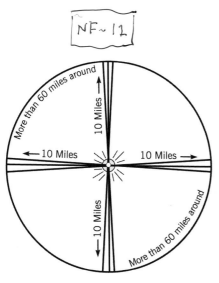

Diagram showing divergence in each of the four beams at Cape Race.

controlled in order for there not to be a loss of light. Another important application of divergence is in sector lights. With some sector lights, a mariner is in the safe channel if the light can be seen. Others are the reverse: the sector light in sight indicates that one is in danger. The width of the beam, or the divergence, is vital to the success of the beacon.

Beams over the water

Every light is restricted in how far it can be seen because of the curved surface of the earth. If you are in a rowboat your eye is very close to the level of the sea and the horizon is only a couple of miles away. If you put a bonfire on a cliff 10m high it can be seen for about 6.6 nautical miles. If on the same cliff you put a light on a tower 20m high (a total of 30m above the sea) the visibility is extended to 11.4 nautical miles. But that's not all. If you are on the bridge of a ship or in the crow's nest on lookout, the effect of your own height above the water is added to that first figure. The normal visibility of Cape Race with its height above the sea at 51.8m, tower plus

cliff, is given in the *List of Lights** at 24 nautical miles. From a very tall ship's lookout to a very high lighthouse the distance of visibility can be as much as 40 nautical miles.

Another odd effect comes into play when a layer of cloud is a couple of hundred metres over the lighthouse. A flashing glare is sometimes visible long before the light itself comes into view, but since the reflection from the cloud is rather diffuse or scattered, it is not nearly as noticeable as the brilliant direct flash of the lighthouse.

*A complete *List of Lights* is published for mariners by the Canadian Coast Guard. The List notes the exact location of each light, its

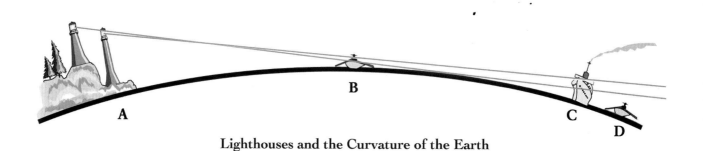

Lighthouses and the Curvature of the Earth

The beams from lighthouses at A are visible to the rowboat at B and the ship at C, but not the rowboat at D

characteristic flashing sequence and the frequency and code of its fog signal. Each light's height above the sea, and the height of the tower itself is included to assist mariners in calculating their distances from lights when they first come into view. Regular updates of this information are provided and new editions are published every few years. (Prior to about 1990, dates of original construction and additions were included.)

Sound

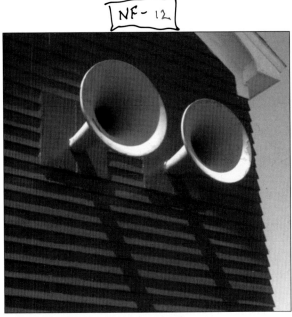

NF-12

Old exterior horns at Cape Race, Nfld.

Fog has long been perilous for sailors. Fog and mist are formed when warm, moist air is cooled as it passes over colder water or as the temperature drops when the sun goes down. The warm Gulf Stream sweeps up the east coast of Canada and meets the cold Labrador Current, causing dense, enduring fogs on Newfoundland coasts, particularly at the Straits of Belle Isle and Cape Race, on the southwest coast of Nova Scotia, and in the Gulf of St. Lawrence. On the west coast of Canada, temperature differences between ocean and air also make for frequent fogs. Even at night, the most powerful beams cannot penetrate fog more than a few metres.

Almost as soon as lighthouses became common in the 17th century, visual aids to navigation were augmented by sounds. At first,

big—if ineffective—bells were installed on lights, tolled by the keepers when fogs "rolled in". Cannon were also tried with erratic results. Reed horns were developed, at first hand-driven and later by steam or compressed air. Sirens and steam whistles were mounted at some stations in the mid-19th century. But it was a Canadian invention, the diaphone, that made controlled sounds consistently audible for many miles.

In diaphones, slotted, hollow pistons move in similarly slotted sleeves in a rapid recip-rocating motion. When the slots meet up, steam escapes, creating sound. Low notes were produced as they penetrate furthest through fog. The combination of a low note followed by an even lower note produces the best results. The move to compressed air diaphones came about 1910. Steam and compressed air diaphones were hard work to run as keepers had to ensure a coal supply on hand, fire up the boilers and maintain the machinery. Diesel-driven air compressors powered later models that lasted until the 1950s and 1960s. While no longer in operation, a few have been preserved such as at Cove Island, Ontario and Bell Island, Newfoundland. In 1999, the diaphone at Estevan Point, B.C. is still in operating order.

After the Second World War, electronic fog horns replaced the old diaphone "groaners".

Electronic Horns (left) & old horn
(right) at Great Duck, Ontario

East Point, P.E.I.

Amphitrite, B.C.

At the same time radar-activated sensors flashed across the sea to detect fog and to turn on their high-pitched squeals. From the start, there were many complaints about the new horns. Sailors had observed that on some days a particular horn could be heard for many miles, while on others, the same horn did not carry at all. Fog absorbs sound waves, particularly those in the higher frequencies of electronic horns. The "erratic" behaviour of fog horns is more likely related to how sound signals are bent as they travel along and between layers of air that are of different temperatures or densities. Submariners long ago recognized this characteristic of sound transmission. Wanting to escape detection by "sonar" (sound activated detectors), they submerged beneath a layer of water of different salinity or temperature.

We often speak of fog as "rolling in". What very often happens is that the fog forms on the spot as the air mass cools. Within a few minutes, clear air can "thicken", then quite suddenly reach the condensation point and form fog. One of the most interesting — and often beautiful — natural features of summer in St. John's, Newfoundland, is to watch the fog forming in the evening. The cool air from the ocean steals into the harbour past the Ft. Amherst lighthouse and on through the narrow entrance to fill the basin beyond with fog. The same phenomenon happens almost every summer evening in Saint John, New Brunswick, and Yarmouth, Nova Scotia. Of course, days and even weeks of grey damp fog on a light station, with the constant wail of the fog horn, are neither very interesting nor beautiful.

Power

In the earliest lighthouses, it was the keeper who carried the oil up the hundred steps or so to keep the lanterns burning. Later it was the keeper who wound the springs or cranked up the heavy weights to the top of the tower to keep the clock-work mechanism turning the lights. When the system broke down it was he or his family who wound the turning mechanism by hand until repairs were made or parts were found. When fog shrouded the shore it was the keeper who cranked the horn or worked the hand bellows.

Steam-driven fog horns were first used on Partridge Island, N.B. lighthouse in 1860. In foggy weather, the keeper had to stoke the furnaces continually. By 1902, the first electrically-operated fog alarm and light had been installed at Cape Croker, Ontario. Diesel engines came after World War I to compress air for fog horns and generate electricity on remote stations, and by the end of the 1930s, electric motors (instead of keeper-wound clockworks) were turning most of the light tables, and supplying the actual light.

Post World War II, main line, hydro-electric power was more and more widespread in Canada, even reaching some island light stations, such as Cove Island, Ontario, via submarine cables. For remote stations and others being destaffed, however, independent power supplies were needed. Diesel generators functioned well enough. But even automatic diesel power stations need maintenence from time to time. Windmill generators were tried at Brandypot Island, but were not very dependable. Solar panels with banks of batteries were the answer and became almost universal in the 1980s and 1990s.

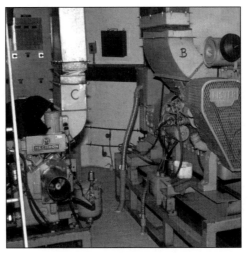

Engine room, Machias Seal, N.B.

Automation

Aluminum lamphouse, Cape Mary's, Nfld.

lighthouse evolution in Canada. In the last 25 years, automation has drastically altered lighthouse operations. The picture of the valiant keeper and his family struggling, in their isolation, to keep the beacon lit is being replaced by the computer-controlled efficiency of empty stations. By 1999, only a few dozen stations in Newfoundland and British Columbia still had staff. Even those small numbers are almost certain to dwindle in the next few years.

Lighthouse automation started a long time ago, as better and better lamps were lasting longer and longer without human attention. High-intensity electric lights such as those using mercury vapour made it possible to

Today, the light station is usually a solitary skeleton tower with brackets to hold fog sensors, electronic fog horns and solar panels, with perhaps one very small service building. The modern, low energy, high efficiency light bulbs are changed automatically by electric power, and fog alarms are turned on and off by computer-controlled switches. Even weather reports are provided by electronic sensors and sent by radio automatically or on remote demand.

At the turn of the 21st century, the automation of lighthouses and the elimination of their keepers and families cap 250 years of

Solar panels (left) & electric horns (centre) at Gull Rock, N.S.

replace the huge Fresnel lenses with smaller, moulded plastic or glass lenses. Not nearly as romantic or beautiful, they were just as effective. A few old-fashioned lamps and weighted clock-works held out into the 1950s, but most stations by this time had switched to electricity, consid-erably cutting down the keeper's workload. In 1953, lightweight, aluminum alloy lamphouses began to replace the earlier cast iron ones. They may not be beautiful, but they are less costly to support and maintain. Many of the graceful old, wooden, tapering pyramids now carry angular, aluminum tops, considerably less stylish than when they supported the octagonal or round, cast iron lamphouses.

Electronic remote control systems started to operate Canadian lighthouse stations by the mid-1960s. Electronic fog horns were being turned on and off by radar detectors around the same time.

Radar came onto the maritime scene during and after World War II. Ships could now see clearly through the densest fogs, no longer blind as they made their way through the channels and rocks in the dark. In the last few years, all vessels, including the smallest pleasure boats, can be equipped with satellite position indicators quite inexpensively. With this equip-ment they can fix their positions anywhere on earth in only a few seconds. Ships need to rely on lighthouses—and keepers—less and less.

After WWII, keepers unions began to form, demanding eight hour days, overtime pay, leave and pension benefits. Normand Lafrenière, writing on lightkeeping on the St. Lawrence, says that it was these demands, more than anything, that hastened the move to automation after World War II. Now most automatic stations are serviced by itinerant technicians.

Lighthouse remains and memorial at Heath Point, Quebec

Keepers

Charles Redhead on Race Rocks, B.C.

Light stations can seem like romantic places, where keepers lead idyllic lives amid beautiful scenery. We see photographs of Peggy's Point lighthouse bathed in a summer sunset; Race Rocks on a calm sunny day; Cape Race on its headland, the breaking seas a white necklace along the rocks. Visitors at Machias Seal Island come to watch the nesting birds. We do not see how it must have been in the long stretches of stormy winter seas, the endless days of shrouding fog, long weeks and months of isolation. We do not see the infrequent visit of supply boats, or the endless struggle to keep warm and dry in insufficient housing.

Through the years, keepers' lives have been as varied as the stations they staffed. On pillar lights and on tiny, bare rock islands, light stations occupy every inch of land. There is

nowhere to go except the balconies of the lights themselves. What a contrast that is to Discovery Island light with its lawns and gardens. Or to Bell Island, Newfoundland, where the keeper and his wife maintain a beautiful summer garden and buy groceries a few minutes away. Point Atkinson near Vancouver, once in isolation, is now within a city park, with buses from downtown.

In the 19th century, keepers lived at the base of the tower, with no telephones, radio or even electricity. Their quarters were cramped, leaky and cold. Smoke was a constant problem with winds making downdrafts in smoky chimneys from the oil lamps of the main light in the same building. On many stations, the only supplies were those rowed out at the beginning of the spring. In the case of life-threatening illness or accident, distress flags were hoisted in hopes of a passing ship. Emergencies might require a dangerous trip across open water. Several dozen keepers were lost on such trips.

As for their duties, oil lamps had to be filled, wicks trimmed or replaced, glass funnels polished and the lenses and reflectors kept spotless. Lamphouse windows had to be cleaned. Weights—running the clockwork mechanisms to turn the rotating lights—had to be wound by hand cranks from the tall towers every three or four hours. Maintenance of the whole station, from minor repairs to the endless painting of steps, walls and buildings, was part of the duty list. Official logs had to be kept up to date. Fog alarms had to be operated in bad weather, at first by hand horns and even by cannon. Later when steam-driven diaphones were introduced, furnaces had to be lit and a supply of coal made ready. Still later, diesel-driven air compressors had to be maintained, started and monitored, to function continuously for up to several days.

Bad weather was a constant source of concern for the keeper and his family. In really big storms stations themselves were in peril from the sea. Over the years, four stations on the west coast were fully or partially destroyed by huge waves. Atlantic storms, and even some in the St. Lawrence, have produced waves that inundated living quarters and reached the tops of the light towers, which shook under the thunderous attack.

Of course, life was not all bad and there was spare time, particularly in good weather. On some stations, gardening, fishing and even hunting added fresh food to the family diet. Reading has always been a mainstay, and in late years, radio and television. The lighthouse sites also offered pastimes. On the north side of Lake Superior, one keeper and his family polished agates from the nearby beaches, and a west coast keeper occupied his spare time making cedar shakes from driftwood logs. Other keepers had bigger dreams in mind. One island keeper built an aircraft. A Department of Transport inspector was flown out occasionally to make the mandatory safety inspections. Another keeper crafted bannister spindles from local wood for his retirement home. On Race Rocks, the keeper built a substantial sailing yacht below the light station for his retirement (see below).

Keepers' wives often began their children's schooling, using Department of Education curricula or devising their own. A few stations were close enough to the mainland to have the children rowed across to nearby schools. Often, though, children from remote stations had to go ashore for months at a time, either to boarding schools or to live with relatives or friends.

Family tradition played a powerful role in the lives of the people of the lights. Children growing up on the lights gradually learned how to carry out the keeper's chores and, along with

Keeper building a boat, Race Rocks, B.C.

Trowbridge Island, Ontario

their mothers, often took over completely for short periods due to accident or illness. Some children found the style of life so natural that their fathers' retirements made them the logical successors. The Lindsays, for example, at Isle Verte, Quebec, kept the light for more than a century, from 1817 to 1964. James Cantwell, the first keeper at Cape Spear, Nfld., did not know when he applied for the job in 1835 that his descendents would carry on there, generation after generation, until the station was automated in the 1960s. The Myricks have been on Cape Race from 1874 until the present. The Fafards kept the light at Pointe des Monts, Quebec, for more than 80 years. Another remarkable record was that of the Georgeson family who tended B.C. lights, notably Active Pass, for several

generations. The first female keeper in Canada, Mary Ann Croft, tended the light on Discovery Island, B.C. for ten years after her father had become incompetent. Upon his death in 1901, she was officially appointed keeper, staying there for another 30 years. Ben Codville spent more than 45 years on the light at Pointer Island on the Inside Passage of the B.C. coast, at first as a child of the keeper, then as his teenaged assistant, and the next 29 years as keeper. It was an astonishing tenure uninterrupted by holidays or trips ashore. Even his wife Ann was a mail order bride.

Over the more than two centuries of Canadian lighthouse history many hundreds of keepers have staffed the lights. The usual variety of human qualities made some succeed while others failed, particularly in early days when appointments were made by political patronage. Self sufficiency and an ability to withstand the isolation were essential, as was a dedication to the safety of those in peril and an ability to improvise. The

Marine traffic control, Amphitrite, B.C.

best keepers were almost all married to devoted and supportive partners.

Improvements of the last fifty years made life on Canadian light stations vastly more comfortable. Electricity brought communications, refrigeration, radio and t.v. Better housing included separate quarters for assistant keepers. Duties became lighter as dependable electric lights needed little attention and electric motors drove the rotating lights and fog horns. Yet at some stations, new functions were added. A few became relay stations for signals from ships. Some had radio beacons installed. Others regularly reported on temperatures and salinities of sea water, and Langara, on the extreme northwest corner of the Queen Charlotte Islands, even became a tsunami (tidal wave) watching station.

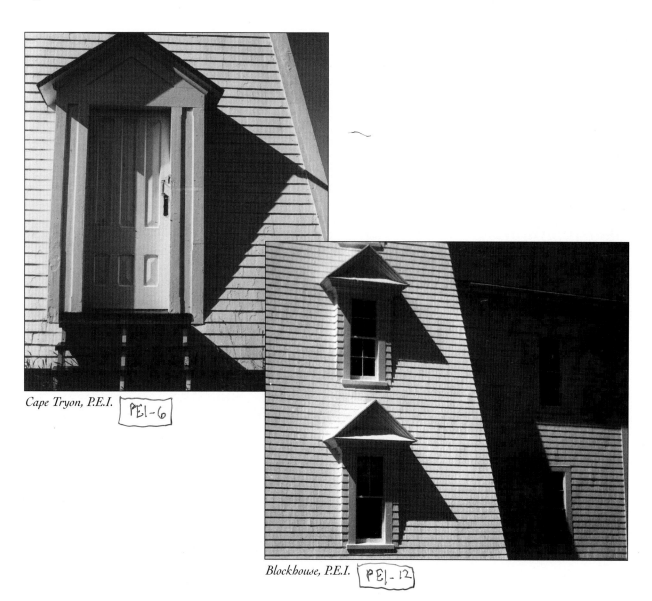

Cape Tryon, P.E.I. PEI-6

Blockhouse, P.E.I. PEI-12

Cape Pine, Newfoundland

NEWFOUNDLAND

For travellers, Newfoundland's nearly 50,000 kilometres of rugged shoreline and its thousands of bays and coves make it a place of great beauty. But it is equally a place of immense natural savagery. Its abrupt cliffs and offshore ledges, its incredible fogs and wild Atlantic storms, have wreaked havoc on ships using the great circle route from Europe to eastern North America and the main routes into Atlantic Canada and the St. Lawrence Seaway from the earliest days of shipping. Since the mid-1400s when the first mariners noted the riches of the surrounding sea, Newfoundland has attracted fishermen from many European maritime countries. As soon as vessels began nearing these shores, they met trouble along the unmarked coasts. Until the introduction of steam power in the mid-19th century, ships sailed under the power of variable winds and were subject to the vagaries of little understood currents and storms which could send them hundreds of miles off course.

By 1830, shipping companies, the Royal Navy and even coastal schooner owners began to plead in London for the construction of lighthouses in the Canadian colonies. When, in the fall of 1839, J.B. Jukes, the first Newfoundland Government geologist, was exploring the shoreline rocks of the southwest corner of Newfoundland, he survived several fierce autumn storms in his small vessel. When the weather cleared after the remains of an Atlantic hurricane, the shoreline was littered with the wrecks of a dozen schooners and ships. Several were lost with all hands. Moved by the devastation, Jukes used the official account of his geological excursions to describe rescues of passengers and crews by local people. One of the residents, George Harvey, saved hundreds of people in his lifetime, and gave them shelter in his home. The Governor General rewarded Harvey's bravery and service with a gold medal and £100.

In his record, Jukes makes a strong observation about the value of lighthouses on the Newfoundland coast:

> I should be unwilling to obtrude my opinion on matters of which I have no professional, and but little practical, knowledge: but surely it seems reasonable that a great commercial nation such as England should not suffer the borders

of the great high-road to Canada and her North American possessions to be thus strewed with the property and bodies of her subjects. A lighthouse on Cape Ray, with a large bell or gun to be used in fogs, together with a smaller lighthouse and a pilot or two, either at Port aux Basques, the Dead Islands, or La Poile, as a harbour of refuge, would be the means of great good.

Newfoundland's geographic position and its indented coastline, both of which have affected its lighthouse history, came from a unique geological history spanning a billion years. Newfoundland was made up of fragments of an ancient continent that once included all the land areas on the globe. As it broke into land masses that we now call North America, Africa and Europe, large slices and irregular pieces were left behind along the east coast of North America. As the ancestral Atlantic Ocean opened, closed and then opened two more times, pieces of continental crust and chunks of old ocean bottom were progressively welded onto the continental edge to make the Newfoundland we know with its strong northeast-southwest grain of headlands and bays. In very recent geological times, the ice cap that covered all of northern North America scraped and scoured out old river valleys and rounded off the hills. The whole area was flooded by rising sea levels in the last 10,000 years, making bays and inlets with bare headlands and low, rounded islands and reefs that today are the settings for lighthouses.

By 1700, fishing armadas set out from Europe every spring to fish the waters off Newfoundland and Labrador. Settlement was prohibited here, but some of the fishermen wintered in sheltered coves and remote places, and thus small villages began. By the early 1800s, local traffic and passing ships on their way to central Canada and the States intensified the need for the lights of which Jukes had written. Cries for navigational aids came from the Royal Navy, shipping companies, vessel owners and merchants, survivors and local governments. And over the years they have been answered; in the 1998 edition of *List of Lights, Buoys and Fog Signals for Newfoundland,* 550 sites are described.

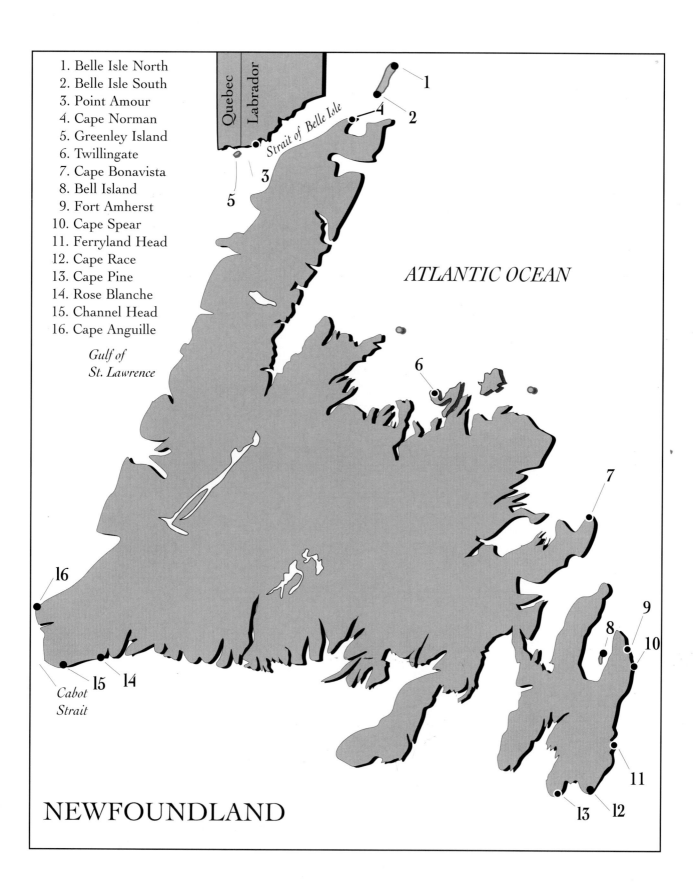

1. Belle Isle North
2. Belle Isle South
3. Point Amour
4. Cape Norman
5. Greenley Island
6. Twillingate
7. Cape Bonavista
8. Bell Island
9. Fort Amherst
10. Cape Spear
11. Ferryland Head
12. Cape Race
13. Cape Pine
14. Rose Blanche
15. Channel Head
16. Cape Anguille

Gulf of St. Lawrence

Quebec

Labrador

Strait of Belle Isle

ATLANTIC OCEAN

Cabot Strait

NEWFOUNDLAND

STRAIT *of* BELLE ISLE *& the* NORTH COAST

Belle Isle North, Newfoundland

Belle Isle North & South

Belle Isle South, Newfoundland

Ships from Europe bound for ports in the St. Lawrence Seaway have a choice of routes. One route follows the great circle a little south of Cape Race where it turns westward through Cabot Strait and into the Gulf of St. Lawrence (see map p.37). Another slightly shorter route passes to the north of the Island of Newfoundland, through the Strait of Belle Isle and into the Gulf.

A logical place to build a landfall light for the northern route was at the south end of Belle Isle. The spot was selected on a headland some 128m (426 ft.) above the sea (see above). Supplies and building materials had to be landed at the base of the steep cliffs, then hauled up to the top of the frightening slopes. The light was in service by 1858 but was soon found to have its own special trouble. Dense fog covers the sea in this area for many days a year. The light was shining high above the weather but out of sight for ships. This lesson had been learned in Europe long before. Because of sea fogs, lights should not be built more than 40m (133 ft.) above the sea.

To compensate at Belle Isle, in 1880 a second light was placed straight down the island's steep escarpment at about 30m (100 ft.) above the water. It was therefore visible under most fogs. It has the same flashing formula as the main light (flash 5 seconds, eclipse 5 seconds). This is certainly one of the shortest lighthouses in Canada: the standard round red lamphouse is set directly onto a flat concrete base with no tower at all.

A wonderful light station, it is set on a spectacular, barren site in view of a procession of ships. It is, however, inaccessible except by sea or helicopter and is completely blocked in late winter and spring by sea ice.

A light station was installed on the north end of Belle Isle in 1905 because some shipping from the Atlantic passes into the Gulf of St. Lawrence by a route to the north of this island. This light was built in the distinctive concrete, flying-buttress style developed by Col. Anderson of the lighthouse service in the first decade of the 1900s. A red lanternhouse and a beaver weathervane sit atop the light. Like the lighthouse at the south end of the island, it is a remote station in a rugged spot and is accessible only with great difficulty.

Belle Isle (North)

Belle Isle (South)

Belle Isle (South)

Point Amour

The tallest lighthouse in Newfoundland at 27.4m (91 ft.) was built in 1857 at Point Amour on the coast of Labrador near the Quebec border. This part of the route from the Atlantic into the Gulf of St. Lawrence was a navigator's nightmare. Until a system of lights provided some assistance, wrecks here were commonplace. The Belle Isle South light to the north, and the Cape Bauld light to the south, bracket the northeast entry to the Strait of Belle Isle. The Cape Norman light is a little farther west along the Newfoundland coast.

Shipwrecks continued along the foggy Labrador coast even after the light at Point Amour was built. The site marks the graves of many ships including two British naval vessels: H.M.S. *Lily* which foundered in fog in 1889 while the lightkeeper worked to save some of the crew; and the cruiser H.M.S. *Raleigh* which in 1922 ran aground in fog with the loss of ten men.

Point Amour light is a round stone tower faced with brick, then cemented and shingled. Its walls are 2m (6.5 ft.) thick at the base and taper slightly. There are eight landings up to the light platform with deep-set windows at each landing. The white tower's daymark is a broad, black, horizontal band about two thirds of the way up and is among the few lights in Canada to use black bands. The round lamphouse has a characteristic outside deck with railing. Its red cupola formerly housed a 2nd Order Fresnel lens system, which has been replaced by an airport-style rotating electric beacon. The substantial duplex keepers' house is two storeys and is joined by a covered passage at the base of the light.

To reach this elegant light, take the highway up the west coast of Newfoundland to the ferry at St. Barbe. It is an hour and a half crossing to Blanc Sablon, Quebec. Local roads running east along the coast lead to the back door in less than an hour. Other notable sights in this area include icebergs in spring and early summer, and an impressive variety of birds and whales in season.

Cape Norman

NF-4

A white, wooden tower with red, rounded lamphouse, a residence and service buildings stood on Cape Norman until they were replaced in 1980. An electronic foghorn replaced the 1880 diaphone in 1971. It continues to bleat its warning out into the Strait slightly west of north.

Roads lead up the west side of Newfoundland to its north end with branch roads leading out to Cape Norman.

Greenly Island

The eyes of the world turned to this remote island a little west of the Quebec border on the Strait of Belle Isle in April 1928, when the lightkeeper's routine wireless weather report had the added words, "German plane". Two days before this laconic message, the airplane *Bremen* with Baron Gunther von Huenefeld, Captain Hermann Koehle and Major James Fitzmaurice aboard had set out from Ireland to try the first westward, trans-Atlantic air crossing. Two days later, fading hopes gave way to despair when there had been no sign of them since takeoff. Navigating by dead reckoning (as required in the days before radio), the men had crossed the coast of Labrador and, thinking that they had gone too far south, turned northward. After a while, they realized their error and turned back southward. Their fuel gauges were falling fast. Spotting a lighthouse and concerned about a snowstorm and the waning daylight, they decided to put down right there. They landed almost completely blind beside the Greenley Island lighthouse and climbed stiffly out of their damaged plane.

A tablet on a big boulder on Greenley Island commemorates the landing of the *Bremen*, an unusual event in the life of the light station. *Bremen* sat comfortably in the Ford Museum in Detroit for many years but has since been returned to Germany. Standing beside the commemorative plaque it's hard to imagine a successful landing during a snowstorm amid the big glacial boulders of Greenley Island.

The first light was installed on Greenley in 1878. It was a 20m (67 ft.), tapering wooden pyramid rising out of one end of the service building and residence. It was surmounted by a round red lamphouse and cupola. Now in its place is a free-standing steel skeleton tower 22m (73 ft.) high. It has a daymark of red lattice work and an automatic searchlight. It now operates on a seasonal basis only.

Twillingate

A boxy, square tower with bevelled shoulders and deep-cut windows supports a concrete platform and lamphouse. Its Fresnel lens system has been replaced by the standard, bull's-eye, rotating searchlight. The tower is located at a windy, rugged site on the north coast of Newfoundland, where covered walkways connect the buildings to protect the keepers from howling Atlantic gales. The light was built in 1876 and modernized in 1980. It is listed as 8.8m (29 ft.) above ground level and 100.9m (336 ft.) above sea level. The half-second flash of its protective beam can be seen every six seconds many miles out into the Atlantic. Its foghorn points almost straight north.

Cape Bonavista

Long headlands and deep bays mark the northeast shore of Newfoundland. The Cape Bonavista headland became a major turning point for coastal navigation around the north coast and so a large light was placed there in 1843. It soon became a north coast landfall light for some European shipping.

The station included a large, square building combining a light tower in the centre of the peaked roof and living quarters for the keepers. Fortunately, the old station, complete with its multiple lamps and polished reflectors, has been restored and is now a Provincial Historic Park. Beside it, a skeletal, steel tower with rotating airport-style beacon performs the lighthouse duties.

Today the white building is painted with bright, red stripes. Inside are the living quarters and the central brickwork that housed the oven and stoves. Most enticing is a look into the light tower where the ancient lamp system is kept in gleaming condition. This apparatus was brought from the famous Bell Rock light, on the east coast of Scotland, after having served there for many years.

AVALON PENINSULA

Ferryland, Newfoundland

Bell Island

One of the best kept lighthouses on the east coast is on the northeast end of Bell Island in Conception Bay, 5 kms (3 mi.) offshore from Portugal Cove. Frequent ferry service back and forth and good roads on the island make this station easily accessible. Bell Island is made up of the youngest rocks on the Avalon Peninsula, reddish sandstones and shales of Ordovician age with several beds of iron ore. These were mined for 70 years until 1966 and in the heyday of mining in the 1940s and 50s produced as much as a million tons a year of hematite ore that was shipped all over the world. Ships came in to docks to be loaded. It was at and near those docks that four ships were torpedoed in two German U-boat attacks in late 1942, killing 69 people.

Even with many large freighters coming and going, no lighthouse was built here until 1940. It was remodelled around 1980 and now consists of a square tower on the corner of a one storey service building. The keeper's house is nearby. Remains of older buildings are visible in the ghosts of foundations in the grass. The light is a fixed omnidirectional lens of the Third Order with a flashing sequence. Power comes from the hydro mains at Bell Island, supplied in turn by submarine cable from Portugal Cove. The lanternhouse is an octagonal, aluminium frame type with flat glass windows. On the seaward side of the building stands the electronic foghorn. The old compressor and air tank are kept in beautiful order by the keeper whose pride in his station is clearly shown by the nicely kept garden and lawns. This beautiful station is easily accessible.

Bell Island omnidirectional Fresnel lens, emergency light to left

Old fog horn at Bell Island

Fort Amherst

Many thousands of visitors look down each year from Signal Hill and Cabot Tower, on the north side of the narrow entrance to St. John's Harbour, and look across to the Fort Amherst light station on the tip of South Head. It is an area full of history, with Cabot Tower itself, the old magazine, 18th-century cannon, the Battery site, and the remains of World War II gun emplacements on both sides of the harbour entrance. But use of this harbour started long before any of these things.

Portuguese fishermen first came to these shores half a century before Columbus first arrived in the Caribbean. By 1700 there were guns and lookouts on the point of the southern head at the entrance to St. John's Harbour with the main fortifications farther in. Until 1772 these guns alternately served French and English military masters as European wars spilled over to North

Fort Amherst lighthouse, St. John's Harbour

America, and Newfoundland changed hands several times. In 1777 (General) Amherst's Tower and Battery were completed as a security and signal station and fort.

The first formal lighthouse in Newfoundland was built in 1811 on the Ft. Amherst site. It was a tower on top of the stone barracks building. It had a simple oil lamp until 1852 when a triple-wick Argand lamp with an annular lens was installed, making it the first dioptric light in Newfoundland. During World War I, some minor fortifications were added and then, in World War II, heavy gun emplacements were built below the light and these still remain. In 1951, the present tower was erected but when the old one was about to be demolished, public outcry stopped all work. For three years, there were two lighthouses at Fort Amherst. But in 1955, the old stone buildings and the light were quietly removed.

Among lighthouses, Fort Amherst and Vancouver Island's Estevan Point share the rare distinction of having been directly under fire during World War II. According to official reports, U-boat 587 stood off St. John's and fired two torpedoes at the St. John's entrance in 1942. One of these exploded just below the guns at the lighthouse but did nothing more than throw up a huge cloud of spray and frighten the surprised garrison.

South Head and the Fort Amherst lighthouse are readily accessible from the South Side dock area and a footpath of a few hundred metres. In addition to the lighthouse and rich history, there is a tearoom in one of the former keeper's cottages.

Cape Spear

NF~10

①In 1836, a large square building with a light cupola on top was completed at Cape Spear, the easternmost point of North America. It was equipped with seven Argand lamps with reflectors that had served at Inchkeith lighthouse on the Scottish coast. Perched on the high point, it was more than 70 metres above the sea and, on clear nights, it was visible for 18 nautical miles.

This beautiful example of an 1830s lighthouse is preserved, restored (although without the old lamps), and maintained as a National Historic Site by Parks Canada. Ten kms (6 mi.) southeast of St. John's, it is easily accessible by road. The light now shines from a rotating bull's-eye searchlight atop an octagonal, concrete tower located closer to the end of the point. Gun emplacements and barracks for the crews, installed below the light in World War II, are accessible along park foot paths.

One of the most remarkable lightkeeping families kept the Cape Spear light from the beginning. On a July day in 1855, the usual summer fog shrouded the coast. The frigate *Rhine* could not find the entrance to St. John's harbour. Eventually a local man, James Cantwell, went out, found the vessel and guided it to safety. Unknown to Cantwell, Prince Henry of Orange was aboard

Cape Spear's cupola

the *Rhine*. He was so grateful that he arranged to grant Cantwell's wish to become the keeper of the Cape Spear light, at that time under construction. There was an added injunction—that the lightkeeping role be passed to succeeding generations of the family. For seven generations, successive Cantwells kept the light at Cape Spear.

Cape Spear's current lighthouse

1830's Cape Spear light, preserved as an historic site

Ferryland Head

The original tower on Ferryland Head (75 kms (47 mi.) south of St. John's) was built of brick in 1871. It was sheathed in steel plates and so it looks somewhat similar to the real cast iron lights that were the fashion in Newfoundland in the late 19th century. The keeper's house was built adjacent to the tower at the same time. Automated long ago and run on domestic hydro, it continues to guide shipping along the coast towards St. John's and northward.

View out lamproom window

Cape Race

From the 18th century onward, Cape Race, on the extreme southeastern corner of Newfoundland, was often the first landfall sighted by mariners on their way from Europe to Canada and the United States. It was known long before that and appears on 16th-century maps as "Cabo Raso", Portuguese for "flat cape". The frequency of wrecks along this coast increased as marine traffic burgeoned in the early 19th century. When several bad wrecks occurred at and near Cape Race in the 1850s, a lighthouse was placed in 1856 on the site of the current light. Made of cast iron with stone foundations and protecting walls, it had a fixed white light produced by 13 lamps with polished metal reflectors. Its location on a headland put the light 55m (180 ft.) above the sea, making it visible in clear weather for about 17 nautical miles.

In the style typical of the day, the living quarters were built around the base of the tower. Also typical of the day were difficulties due to decisions that were taken in far away London. Take the materials used in construction, for example. Inside the cast iron towers, built at several places in

Newfoundland, condensation was constant. In winter, the residences were often lined with hoar frost. Local authorities complained bitterly, but separate living quarters built of brick and wood were not approved for many years.

The new light on Cape Race was a wonderful help to seafarers but wrecks continued, if somewhat less frequently. In December 1856, within the first year of operation, *Welsford* hit the rocks below the light. *Welsford* went down with her entire crew except for four men whom the lightkeepers managed to drag ashore and up the cliffs to safety. In April 1863, *Anglo Saxon* crunched onto the jagged rocks a few thousand feet down the coast in a dense fog, broke her back and sank, losing 237 passengers and crew. In October of the same year, *Africa*, another passenger liner, fell victim to the same rugged shoreline. A current map citing known wrecks shows 360 names along the coastline around Cape Race. The keepers and their helpers had to be constantly alert for wrecks, but in most cases, the seas and shorelines were too difficult to do much but assist those who managed to get ashore. When *Assyria* crashed into nearby rocks in June 1901, most did manage to get ashore. Her massive anchor turned up years later and now rests on the grass outside the keeper's quarters.

Nothing could be done about the dense fogs and dirty weather on this strategic corner where ships turned from their trans-Atlantic courses. But a more powerful light with a sharper, narrower beam would help, and so would a fog horn. Within a few years of the first lighthouse construction, it became apparent that each light needed to be identified more precisely. Following the trend in other parts of the world, a rotating mechanism was installed at Cape Race in 1866 to make a characteristic flashing pattern possible. The year 1872 brought the installation of a throaty steam whistle, which boomed out over the sea. Like all fog horns, in calm weather it could be heard for many miles but in more turbulent air, it was audible for only three or four nautical miles. Today, electronic sounds have replaced the great bull horns of earlier times. Pieces of rusting boilers and cinder heaps are about all that remain of the old days.

The original tower and lights, improved from time to time as fuels and lamps improved, lasted until 1907 when the present magnificent structure was built. Some say that the original light tower was moved to Cape North, at the tip of Cape Breton Island, in order to replace an old wooden structure. The British authorities had just turned over the Cape Race light to the Canadian Government. The Canadian authorities realized the inadequacies of the old light, and with the increase in shipping, they saw the need for a new and more powerful signal.

Canada built an enormous, reinforced, concrete tower 6m (20 ft.) in diameter and nearly 30m (100 ft.) tall. A spiral stairway, attached to the inside walls, leads to a cast iron collar supporting a lantern room with a rivetted copper dome surmounted by a round ball and weather vane. The "hyperradial" lens system (see page 57) was the largest and finest available at the time. It has four faces, each nearly 4m (13 ft.) high and throwing its own beam. On a foggy night you would be able to see all four beams going round like spokes in a wheel.

"Hyperradial" describes the few lens systems that were right off the scale of those used for most lights, which ranged from Sixth Order (the smallest) to the First Order. Only a few of the huge and powerful hyperradials were ever built and they are landmarks wherever they are: at the famous Bishop's Rock in the U.K., in France, China, and near Karachi, Pakistan. Nearly half a ton of mercury is used at Cape Race to "float" the seven tons of glass in the lens system plus the weight of the metal frames. With its four great lens panels revolving once each 30 seconds, a mariner could see the light flash for three tenths of a second every seven and a half seconds, and then flash again. Cape Race is the only light of this kind in this part of the world. In 1998, the old clockwork mechanism for turning the light and the massive weights to run the clockwork were still in place, however, the light is now being turned by a quietly humming, electric motor.

Ships from Europe or travelling eastbound passed close to shore and would sometimes pick up or drop off passengers and mail. Newfoundlanders would come to Cape Race to catch the fast mail boats offshore. At one time, the Associated Press of New York stationed a boat nearby to meet the liners coming from England and to collect the latest European news in cannisters dropped from the ships. Cape Race had connections to the telegraphic network and from here the European news reached New York and Boston long before the ships did. Perhaps Cape Race is remembered more than anything for its Marconi station which picked up distress signals from *Titanic* in the early days of wireless. The Titanic's remains lie some 3,600m (12,000 ft.) below the water's surface to the southeast of Cape Race.

In 1957, when *Stockholm* rammed and sank *Andrea Doria* off the New England coast, Cyril Myrick was at the radio on Cape Race, relaying messages from rescue ships. Members of the Myrick family had staffed that station since 1874, a noteworthy family dynasty. Cyril Myrick in a 1998 interview in the *St. John's Telegram* recalls when he was a school boy, having watched convoys passing nearby in World War II. H.M.C.S. *Valleyfield*, a Canadian corvette, was sunk by submarine in 1944 just off Cape Race.

This great landfall light on its bare headland is a magnificent sight in fine weather. However, the view is cut to a few metres in overcast weather, when notoriously dense fogs cloak the sea and land for about a third of the days every year. In late winter and early spring, sea ice ordinarily drifts in tight against the rocks of the Cape closing off all navigation. With spring or autumnal gales bringing driving rain or snow on winds well over a hundred miles an hour, it is no wonder the lighthouse tower walls are so thick and strong.

Cape Race was declared a National Historic Site in 1974, but as at nearby Cape Pine, it awaits some real action to preserve this wonderful light in its historic spot. It is readily accessible by car southward from St. John's in a little over three hours.

Cape Race tower

The "smoking chimney" stamp. A philatelic flaw on the top right stamp has smoke coming from a service building to the left of the Cape Race tower. Note the standard stamp below it which has no "smoking chimney."

Cape Pine

By 1850, it was absolutely essential to build lighthouses on the south coast of Newfoundland. After all, this was the north side of the main entrance to the Gulf of St. Lawrence, and as geologist Jukes noted in 1840, the south coast was littered with wrecked ships and often strewn with bodies. After debating responsibility with Newfoundland and Canada, His Majesty's Government in London finally agreed to build a lighthouse on Cape Pine on the south end of the Avalon Peninsula, close to the southernmost point of Newfoundland. Cape Pine was not a descriptive name for the chosen headland, with its generally barren landscape.

At Cape Pine, construction materials included cast iron plates to bolt together on site, a Chance Brothers lamphouse, a platform, and a lens system. Shipped from Britain to a landing site below the lighthouse, pieces were lugged up the cliffs and assembled into the structure that stands to this day. The damp, cold and foggy climate plagued this cast iron light and its living quarters. Condensation, hoar frost and leaks eventually forced the building of separate living quarters.

The light started service on January 1, 1851 with 16 Argand burners and reflectors rotating to produce a recognizable flashing beacon. In 1928, the fuel was changed to acetylene gas and then, in 1961, the light began receiving power from the local hydro system. Now it is an automated station with a simple rotating searchlight in the original tower, equivalent to a 2nd Order light of the old style, and an electronic foghorn calling out across the foggy waters. The keepers' houses have been boarded up. The *List of Lights* notes that the station is 14m (47 ft.) above the ground and 96m (320 ft.) above the sea with a horn that points close to due south.

Cape Pine Light has been designated an Historic Site but, in 1998, it was still awaiting overdue restoration and maintenance. Resident sheep, wandering caribou and occasional tourists are the only visitors. It is easily accessible by car, about four hours drive south from St. John's. Its three red horizontal bands make an impressive barber pole daymark, from land or sea.

WEST COAST *from* ROSE BLANCHE

Cape Anguille, Newfoundland

Rose Blanche

Community of Rose Blanche

In 1873, an unusual stone lighthouse and residence were built all in one block at Rose Blanche near the southwest corner of Newfoundland. The Rose Blanche community, 40 kms (25 mi.) east of Port aux Basques, takes its name from *roche blanche*, French for "white rock".

The beam from the original lighthouse at Rose Blanche Point was about 30m (100 ft.) above sea level, so it must have been visible at sea to the southward for at least ten or twelve nautical miles, more than adequate for fishermen and useful to coastal shipping.

Roberts, an Englishman, became the first keeper in 1873. The lamps he maintained are reputed to have come from Scotland, as Scottish lighthouses were being modernized. After Roberts' tenure, five other families tended the light, until it was decommissioned in the 1940s. Descendants of those families still live in Rose Blanche and nearby communities.

An engraving from 1873 shows a two-storey, square house built of large rectangular blocks of stone, deep set windows in thick walls and a light tower as an upward extension of one of the corners. At roof level, the tower starts out square and the masonry on the four corners is cleverly bevelled in order to make it octagonal for the lamphouse. At the top is a plain octagonal lamphouse with flat sheets of glass sloping inward to an octagonal cupola.

After it was decommissioned, the old stone edifice was abandoned and fell into ruin. Only the tower still maintained its shape; the old cupola and lamphouse window frames were a trifle bent but were still in place. Beginning in 1996, the Southwest Coast Development Association (SWCDA), a non-profit organization encouraging economic and cultural development, began a project to restore the old building and tower. The SWCDA obtained assorted grants for the project, including training grants to assist local people to become masons. As part of the painstaking effort to restore the buildings, fallen stones in the ruins were catalogued and cleaned. Old photographs were enlarged and individual blocks recognized and numbered. About 70% of the original stone blocks were recovered and used in the restoration. Lost stones were replaced from a quarry, opened near the original one, and hauled up to the site by hand. The old building and tower now stand much as they did when they were first built in 1873.

The Association's ultimate aim is to have a focal point for tourism in this area of superb ocean scenery. A walking park is planned leading to the restored, old lighthouse at the end of the point. Lighthouse lovers and those interested in the cultural history of Newfoundland will applaud their efforts. Meanwhile, nearby, a white, square, skeleton tower with an automated rotating light provides a beacon for those at sea.

Channel Head NF-15

In 1875, a light station was placed on Channel Head near the entrance to Port aux Basques Harbour, on the southwestern corner of the Island of Newfoundland. When the Newfoundland Railway was completed in 1894, Port aux Basques became its southwestern terminus and the principal entry and exit point for travel to Newfoundland from the mainland. Passengers and freight crossed the narrowest part of Canso Strait to and from North Sydney, Nova Scotia. A century later, the Newfoundland Railway is but a memory. Today a modern fleet of ferry ships, carrying up to 350 cars each, maintain a year-round service connecting the highway systems of Newfoundland and mainland Canada.

Now hundreds of thousands of people are able to see Channel Head, with its slender, white lighthouse tower. It was built to complement another station at Cape Ray, 12 miles around the corner, NF-19 which was constructed by Canada in 1871. The two lights were to bracket the entry to the Cabot Strait with St. Paul's Island, off the north tip of Cape Breton. The original lighthouse was of circular iron construction and lasted until it was replaced in 1980 by the modern set up. The current light tower is 7.8m (26 ft.) high and has a red band daymark, radio masts and service buildings. Its booming diaphone fog horn was installed early in the twentieth century and lasted until it was replaced by an electronic horn in 1980.

Cape North, Nova Scotia

NOVA SCOTIA

Nova Scotia is a province of coastlines, each one distinctive and posing its own different problems for the navigator and the lighthouse builder. Cape Breton's bold cliffs give way eastward to the shallow, sandy bottomed Northumberland Straits shoreline all the way to the New Brunswick border. The southeast shore from Cape Breton to Yarmouth is an irregular shoreline with bays and inlets, thousands of islands and reefs offshore and, at Halifax, one of the finest natural harbours in the world. This sawtooth shoreline is open to the full fury of gales sweeping in from the Atlantic, with 50ft waves not uncommon in the storm season. The Gulf Stream, a huge river of warm ocean water sweeping up the east side of North America, meets Labrador's south-flowing, icy current off Newfoundland and Nova Scotia. It is an ideal place for fog to form, sometimes lasting many weeks.

From Brier Island to Camp Split (250 kms) the dark basaltic cliffs of the Bay of Fundy offer little shelter other than at Digby Gut. Everyday, inside the Minas Basin, the highest tides in the world roll in to flood the extensive red mud flats. Here, millions of tons of gypsum are shipped out each year from Avonport in vessels that must come and go "on the tide."

No lighthouses graced the Nova Scotian coasts for 150 years after Champlain first wintered at Annapolis in 1604. The first lighthouse in Canada was built at Louisbourg in 1734 to serve naval and military needs. Halifax grew rapidly in the early 18th century. A flood of small ships carrying immigrants, trading goods, and supplies for the Royal Navy base, necessitated the building of Sambro Island lighthouse in 1760 at the mouth of the harbour. Farther down the coast, shore lights were built at Cape Roseway (1788) and Shelburne (1789), along with a dozen more in the next 20 years. By this time, lighthouses for local traffic were in construction in many small harbours. They were mainly simple wooden structures with oil lamps of limited range, which burned local fuels such as seal or fish oil. By the mid-19th century, major lights had been established at vital locations such as Cape Forchu, and Brier and Seal Islands, on the southeast shore.

All along the sea coast of Nova Scotia, tiny fishing villages sprang up in the sheltered coves. Some villages stayed small while others, such as Yarmouth, Shelburne and Lunenburg, grew into major fishing centres. As settlement developed along with coastal trade and growing naval activity, so did the construction of aids to navigation. In the Coast Guard's 1998 *List of Lights*, Nova Scotia has several hundred aids, lighthouses, range lights, buoys, and channel markers listed. The lighthouses are all automated now and either receive their power from the mainland grid or solar power. Even on the foggy coasts of Nova Scotia it does not require a very large solar array to produce enough power to run a modern light and electronic horn.

Nova Scotians can take special pride in their contribution to the advancement of lighthouse technology. In 1846, Dr. Abraham Gesner, a physician from Cornwallis, invented a technique for distilling kerosene from coal. The light at Maugher's Beach, at the mouth of Halifax Harbour, was the first to try the new fuel for lamps in 1851. A vast improvement, Gesner's fuel was quickly adopted at most Canadian and many foreign light stations. For decades it remained the fuel of choice for oil lamps and its use persisted at a few Canadian lights into the 1950s.

At the end of the 20th Century, all traditional lightkeepers are gone from the coasts of Nova Scotia. Crews of technicians, helicopter pilots and specialist engineers have taken their place. Many light stations are being saved and restored by interested people in associations and societies dedicated to preserving the lighthouses for generations to come.

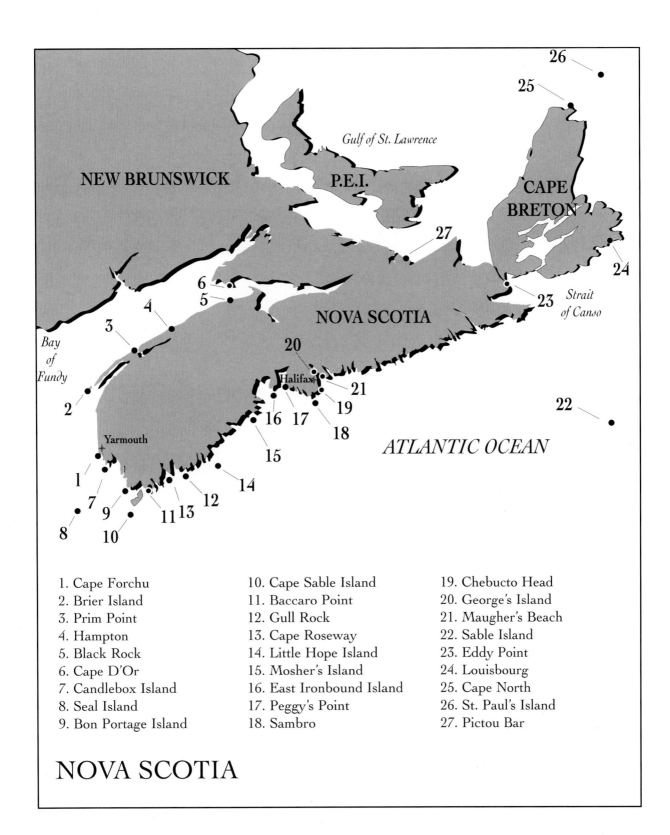

Gulf of St. Lawrence

NEW BRUNSWICK

P.E.I.

CAPE BRETON

26

25

27

24

23

Strait of Canso

NOVA SCOTIA

Bay of Fundy

ATLANTIC OCEAN

22

6

5

4

3

20

Halifax

21

19

18

17

16

2

Yarmouth

1

7

9

8

10

11

13

12

14

15

1. Cape Forchu
2. Brier Island
3. Prim Point
4. Hampton
5. Black Rock
6. Cape D'Or
7. Candlebox Island
8. Seal Island
9. Bon Portage Island

10. Cape Sable Island
11. Baccaro Point
12. Gull Rock
13. Cape Roseway
14. Little Hope Island
15. Mosher's Island
16. East Ironbound Island
17. Peggy's Point
18. Sambro

19. Chebucto Head
20. George's Island
21. Maugher's Beach
22. Sable Island
23. Eddy Point
24. Louisbourg
25. Cape North
26. St. Paul's Island
27. Pictou Bar

NOVA SCOTIA

YARMOUTH
to the head of
BAY *of* FUNDY

Cape Forchu, Nova Scotia

Cape Forchu

Cape Forchu

Travellers on the ferries between Nova Scotia and Maine pass in front of Cape Forchu light on the outer reaches of Yarmouth Harbour. Serving local shipping, the light also points the way into the Bay of Fundy, as do Seal Island light to the south and Brier Island light to the north. A fine, wooden, octagonal tower was built on the point in 1839. It had a Chance Brothers lamphouse and 2nd Order Fresnel lens. In 1962, the old tower was replaced by a slender 22.9m (70 ft.), reinforced-concrete tower and airport-style beacon with the same red and white vertical striped daymark as the old wooden tower. Cape Forchu is now equipped with dual electronic horns that blow in unison. For a while, this site became the monitoring station for the many automated stations in southeast Nova Scotia but that function was transferred to L'Etite, N.B. in 1993. The Fresnel lens from Cape Forchu is on display at the Yarmouth County Museum.

At one time, Cape Forchu's light was accessible only by water, but the island can now be reached easily from Yarmouth by road and causeway. The neat grounds and gardens are impressive, and the former keeper's house is now a museum of the lighthouse's history. The Friends of the Yarmouth Museum are dedicated to preserving the light station and the area's history, going back to the early Portuguese explorers. The light itself still flashes (although less powerfully) and local boaters find the horn a useful tool in the frequent fogs.

Canada is indeed fortunate that private groups all over the country are undertaking to save historic light stations and make them available to visitors. Cape Forchu is an excellent example of what can be done.

Old Cape Forchu

Brier Island

In 1603, Samuel de Champlain's ship was the first marine traffic in the Bay of Fundy. Starting in the 1770s, a flood of Loyalists came north from New England and, in 1783, founded the City of Saint John. As traffic grew, so did the need for lighthouses. One of the earliest was an impressive light completed on Brier Island, at the southern tip of Digby Neck in 1809. The original wooden tower was replaced in 1944 by this reinforced-concrete, octagonal tower with flaring concrete platform and aluminum lamphouse. The light source, originally oil lamps, went through the usual evolution from wicks to mantles and now mainland electricity. The daymark is three red bands against the white tower.

Brier Island is a spectacular spot with the sea all around its black basaltic rocks. It is readily accessible by taking Nova Scotia Route 217 from Digby, then crossing two narrow "guts" by ferries equipped to handle fierce tidal currents. Once on the island, follow the road to the end. The lighthouse sits astride the great flushing tides of Fundy. Rich in nutrients, the waters here entice schools of small fish, seabirds, dolphins and whales.

Point Prim

Digby Gut is the entry into Annapolis Basin, a protected bay on an otherwise exposed coast. It has been an entry point into this part of Nova Scotia for hundreds of years. Indians chose their travel days carefully when canoeing across the 69 km (43 mi.) Bay of Fundy from the mouth of the St. John River. In 1604, Champlain came in through the narrow "gut" and founded a settlement at Annapolis Valley, one of the earliest in North America. By 1817, commerce and settlement justified a lighthouse on the west side of the entrance at Point Prim. A standard, square, wooden residence with tower on top was equipped with oil lamps and reflectors. Its replacement in the 1870s began the daymark tradition of a broad, vertical, red stripe. The modern automated and unstaffed light is a square, concrete tower on the corner of a service building, its daymark a broad, red, vertical stripe on each seaward face.

Passengers on the Saint John-Digby ferry can see this lighthouse on their way in and out of Digby. It is also readily accessible from a side road that meets the ferry terminal road from the town of Digby.

Hampton

The Fundy shore of Nova Scotia is marked by low cliffs from Digby northeastward to Cape Split. Here and there, small coves and inlets provide partial shelter for fishing boats. One of these is at Hampton on the Fundy coast parallel to Bridgetown. Take Exit 20 from the main Highway 101 through the Annapolis Valley. Built in 1911, the neatly painted, tapering, square tower sits slightly back from the sea. The seascape is typical of tidal Fundy. At high tide, boats nod at their collars in the full harbour, but a few hours later, with the tide out, they are stranded on the mud and gravel bottom.

Port George

Port George is another of the small coves and harbours on the Fundy shore, opposite Middleton on NS 101 (Exit 18). The shore road runs alongside this small pepperpot lighthouse. The Bay of Fundy's tidal waters are within a few meters and boats are drawn up alongside. Margaretsville light is just along the road to the northeast.

Cape D'Or

Cape D'Or, on the north side of Minas Channel, witnesses the surges of the world's highest tides. It sits on a point of dark, volcanic rocks of Triassic age (when dinosaurs began) and at high tide is surrounded by water. Low tide, six hours later, reveals expanses of dark rocks, kelp and a few boulders on beaches below the cliffs. The light still guides shipping in and out of Minas Basin, including a few local boats, and ocean-going freighters carrying rock gypsum from Windsor, N.S. to ports along the eastern U.S. seaboard. At high tide captains tie up at Avonport docks with 12m (40 ft.) of water beneath them. At low tide, the ships sit on the soft reddish muddy bottom, waiting for the next tide to take them out to sea.

Cape D'Or is a modest station. Automated long ago, it now has a summer tea room. The light is accessible by a side road from the coastal road west from Parrsboro, N.S.

YARMOUTH *to* HALIFAX

Betty Island, Nova Scotia

Candlebox Island

After visiting the major light at Seal Island on the southern tip of Nova Scotia, our helicopter was heading back to the mainland when the pilot banked to the left and started to talk amusedly about something he wanted to show me on Candlebox Island. The pilot could hardly contain his glee as he described the island below and its athletic occupant. The island was a treeless few acres with a house on one side and a small undistinguished lighthouse on the other. However, there was a clearly visible path around the island's circumference. As the story goes, once every day, the keeper came out in his jogging shoes and ran around and around his tiny empire until completing his required number of laps. Looking down from the circling helicopter, all I could think of was poet, William Cowper's words, "I am monarch of all I survey... from centre all round to the sea...."

Seal Island

Tamarack "knees"

It started around 1820 near the extreme southwest corner of Nova Scotia. Two families, the Crowells and the Hickens, settled on Seal island to do a little farming and to aid distressed mariners who were being cast ashore there in growing numbers. When accidents increased, petitions went forth and by 1830 a lighthouse was built. The Crowells and Hickens were joint keepers.

The lighthouse remains a fine example of frame construction of the period. Tamarack "knees" were used in the lighthouse for support. Single pieces of wood cut from the bases of tamarack trees, tamarack "knees" were commonly used in Maritime shipbuilding for their strength. The tapering, octagonal tower is shingled and painted white, its daymark two broad, red horizontal bands. When I first visited Seal Island in 1979, the original Chance Brothers' cast-iron lanternhouse with its 2nd Order Fresnel lens was still in service. These were replaced in 1980 by an octagonal aluminum lamphouse and an airport beacon light. The original glass lens is now on display in a partial replica of the Seal Island lighthouse, administered by a local museum in Barrington, on the mainland opposite Seal Island.

Today, the diesel generators are hard at work for their computer masters. Even they will soon be replaced by solar panels and banks of batteries. The light atop the old timbered tower guides the way in and out of the Bay of Fundy and along the Nova Scotia shores.

*Seal Island lens &
lamphouse in a replica
at Barrington on
Highway 2*

Seal Island, N.S.

Keeper at Seal Island, N.S.

Bon Portage Island

Who could have guessed in 1874 that this modest, four-sided light tower would one day become so widely known? It did not begin that way at the light station on the south end of Bon Portage Island. For the first 55 years, life was routine. The change of seasons was the principal event. Keepers came and went. Occasionally there was a shipwreck nearby. And always there were ships and boats to serve. In 1898, the steamship *Express* went ashore just below the light and slowly disintegrated, leaving bits of rusted steel among the boulders on the shore. Then, in 1926, Morrill Richardson and his new wife, Evelyn, bought the 700-acre island to run a small farming operation. Richardson nurtured hopes that he would one day become lightkeeper, and in the spring of 1929, the job was his. The young couple moved to the dilapidated station on the undeveloped island.

For the next fifteen years, the Richardsons worked hard fixing up the leaky, draughty buildings. They cleared and improved the land, and raised their family. There were oil lamps and a wood stove, no running water, and outdoor plumbing only. Communication with the outside world required a trip in a small boat across open ocean. In case of emergency, they would raise a flag on the lighthouse to alert friends on the mainland. In the dead of winter, sea ice sometimes blocked them off completely for weeks at a time. Yet for all this, they had a good family life, lived close to nature and had enough, in a material sense, to get by. Evelyn Richardson wrote about their life in a wonderful, sensitive book, *We Keep a Light*, which became a best-seller and won the Governor General's Award in 1945.

The old leaky tower and house are long gone, replaced by a square, concrete tower with electric light and modern keepers' houses. Instead of the original, hand-driven horn, an electronic signal is activated by a radar detector and computer-controlled switches. The Richardsons' hard-won fields, the pathways along the shore beside the saltwater ponds, the wind-blown woods where they loved to walk... all these are now a bird sanctuary. A research station occupies the keepers' former residence. Even the name has changed from Bon Portage to Outer Island.

Bon Portage or Outer Island light station is accessible by boat from Shag Harbour and is visible from some spots there, notably the grounds of the Evelyn Richardson Memorial School.

Cape Sable

Long sand and gravel spits sweep southward from Clark's Harbour to form the southernmost point of Nova Scotia and a hazard to navigation. After the *Hungarian* was lost with all hands off Cape Sable in a winter storm in early 1860, the Government of Nova Scotia decided to build a light station on the point. Lit in 1861, it proved effective in reducing the number of wrecks.

The existing concrete tower is nearly a hundred feet (28m) high, slender, white and tapering. The electric lamp and lens system in the red, octagonal lamphouse sends out a beam visible for up to 24 kms (15 mi.) depending on the fog. The notorious fogs sometimes last for weeks. Unlike Sable Island, where several miles have been eroded from its east end over the last 150 years, Cape Sable's curving spits and bars are fairly stable with only minor accretion and erosion.

The station was destaffed in 1986 and the out-buildings burned in 1988, leaving this beautiful tower alone on the site. While it is visible from the beach at The Hawk, below Clark's Harbour, the lighthouse is accessible only by boat.

Baccaro Point

Baccaro in fog.

Baccaro Point, on the east side of the entrance to Barrington Bay in Shelburne County, is the southernmost point on the Nova Scotia mainland and, surprisingly, a few minutes of latitude farther south than Toronto. Lighthouses on Seal Island and Cape Sable Island, not far to the east, are even farther south.

A lighthouse was built on Baccaro Point in 1850 long before roads reached that far. Construction materials had to be hauled along the beaches to the boulder-strewn granite point as it was impossible to land at the point. The original lighthouse was replaced by the present structure in 1976. It is a square tower, 13.4m (45 ft.) high with an octagonal lanternhouse. Inside, an omnidirectional lens with a winking electric bulb gives its characteristic three flashes every ten seconds. Its electronic foghorn, on a separate stand near the tower, points southward out to sea with a two-second blast every 20 seconds.

When I visited Baccaro in 1980, the lighthouse was almost lost in a complex defense establishment with radar domes and support buildings. When I visited again in 1998, the automated light stood by itself, alongside the broken foundations of the keeper's house and the service buildings. On that visit, the lighthouse point was right on the edge of a fogbank that drifted in and out, on and off the land. Especially dramatic was the sound of heavy engines as a large fishing boat passed the point, invisible in the fog but close by and presumably listening to the Baccaro warning signals. A local road leads to the site from Port La Tour, just off the old coastal Route 109 to a parking and picnic area. A sign warns the unwary not to stand too close to the bank of fog horns, a few metres from the tower. They sound without warning whenever the radar sensors detect fog some distance offshore.

Lockeport (Gull Rock)

A rectangular concrete dwelling, with square, concrete tower emerging from the roof occupies the highest spot on a wave-swept, granite island (Gull Rock) on the south coast of Nova Scotia. It is the largest among several reefs and tiny islands in the centre of the entry channel into Lockeport Harbour, about 5 kms (3 mi.) south of Lockeport village. In earlier times, there were two auxiliary buildings beside the main one, but by 1998, these had disappeared, leaving only debris-cluttered, concrete foundation walls.

The light with its red octagonal lanternhouse has been on Gull Rock since 1853. It used various lamps over the years, but now uses an electric bulb. An omnidirectional lens has a complicated but immediately recognizable pattern: flash 17 seconds, eclipse 5 seconds, flash 3 seconds eclipse 5 seconds. Power for the light and the electronic horns is supplied by an array of solar cells on a small platform partway up one side of the building (see p.28).

This station is not very accessible, requiring a boat and a period of the perfectly calm weather that is so rare in the area. It can be seen in the distance from the end of the road on Western Head, four kms (2.5 mi.) south of Lockeport village.

Cape Roseway

The third lighthouse in Nova Scotia, Cape Roseway, on McNutt's Island, was built of stone quarried on site in 1788. According to local lore, even the mortar - made by burning mussel shells - was made on the island. The light's first lamp burned seal oil, and the first fog signal - installed in 1831- was a cannon (as was common at that time). The old light was replaced in 1977 by an octagonal concrete tower with white platform, red railings and octagonal lamphouse. Some 17.7m high (59 ft.) on a base 16.1m (54 ft.) above sea level, the light is visible for 16 miles. Its deep-voiced diaphone boomed out over the sea into the fog until 1972 when electronic horns were installed.

In 1998, dilapidated service buildings and keepers' houses lay boarded up. This station is accessible from Gunning Cove by boat, then a three km (1.9 mi.) walk across the island.

Little Hope

No more than a patch of boulders a couple of metres above sea level, Little Hope Island has room to spread one's wings, but little else. It is about 16 kms (10 mi.) from Liverpool and 3 kms (1.9 mi.) off-shore. Its 25m (80 ft.) concrete tower with modest buttresses supports a small light run from solar panels.

Mosher's Island

A white, circular tower stands on Mosher's Island, on the west side of the entrance to La Have River just south of Lunenburg. A square, pyramidal wooden tower was built here in 1868 and lasted more than a century. In 1999 little remains but the "new" automated tower. The site is only accessible by boat from Dublin Shore or nearby. This photograph was taken in 1989 after the new tower had been installed but before the old one was demolished.

East Ironbound Island

Part of the string of coastal lights south and west of Halifax Harbour, this 12m (40 ft.) square tower rises like an oversized church steeple out of a small, two storey, oblong dwelling. Built in 1867, the tower has white shingles, bright red roof, lantern platform and a polygonal lamphouse. Festoons of supporting cables give it a unique charm. This automated tower is only accessible by sea or helicopter.

Peggy's Point

A lighthouse was built on Peggy's Point at the east side of the entrance to St. Margaret's Bay in 1868. It was one of a series of lighthouses built on outer points to ease navigation along the southeast coast of Nova Scotia. It was replaced in 1979 by the existing structure: a tapering, octagonal, concrete tower, 15.2m (50 ft.) high. Its base sits on the bare, massive granite rock of the Point. Its aluminum lamp-house has flat glass panes. Inside, an omnidirectional lens provides a wide arc of light out to the sea.

Known to millions as "Peggy's Cove" light owing to the small, picturesque fishing village nearby, it is readily accessible on Route 333, 40 kms (25 mi.) from Halifax. In summer the area teems with tourists from all over the world. A post office has been built into the base of the lighthouse so that tourists can have their mail cancelled with a Peggy's Cove cachet. This modest lighthouse has become the most popular attraction in the province. In September of 1998, Peggy's Point hosted a flood of the world's press, family and rescuers in the aftermath of the Swissair Flight 111 crash, in which 229 lives were lost only five miles offshore. The lighthouse appeared in media coverage all over the world.

Sambro Island

The oldest serving lighthouse in Canada, and likely North America, stands on a glacially-rounded, granite island at the entrance to Halifax Harbour. Several old cannon tell of its strategic military importance in Canada's early history. In 1758, the Nova Scotia legislature provided for the construction of a lighthouse on Sambro Island by levying taxes on "spirits" and then on passing ships. The government of Nova Scotia even conducted a lottery in 1758 to raise money for the light. In 1760, a sixty-foot stone tower was completed and its beacon first shone forth over the troubled waters.

By 1769 something was clearly wrong. Captain after captain complained he could not see the Sambro light. The nearby wreck of H.M.S. *Granby* in 1771 brought things to a crisis. Rules and equipment were changed. New locally developed lamps were installed that did not smoke up the lantern glazing. The light source followed the usual evolution through different fuels including the new kerosene from coal invented by Nova Scotian, Abraham Gesner (p. 91), Argand lamps, mantle-vapour lamps, and finally electricity.

In 1907, another 6.2m (20 ft.) was added to the original 18.6m (60 ft.) tower. In 1969, the beautiful old Bernier lamphouse and Fresnel lens of the 2nd Order were replaced by an angular, aluminum top with a rotating, airport-type beacon. Red bands mark the white tower, which is topped by a red lanternhouse. The original lens is on public view at the Nova Scotia Museum in Halifax. In earlier days, Sambro was an isolated station even though it was close to a city. More recently, keepers had radio and TV, electric utilities, and sent their children to nearby mainland schools.

Sambro Island light stands at the entrance to Halifax Harbour, one of the busiest ports on the eastern seaboard. It has witnessed naval and mercantile history from the early days of sailing ships to today's enormous container ships and cruise liners. With their radar and satellite position indicators, ships now only glance at Sambro as they pass. Still, Sambro remains a useful light for an island and reef-studed coast with deep indentations, tricky ocean currents and stormy seasons. After nearly two and a half centuries, Sambro continues to send out its warning signals. Now automated, it is accessible by boat.

Chebucto Head

The masts and antennae of Chebucto Head light station, on the west side of the entrance to Halifax Harbour, indicate a thorough range of modern aids to navigation. Chebucto Head is also part of Halifax Control, monitoring traffic in and out of this world-ranking port. During both World Wars, thousands of ships assembled in Halifax Harbour and adjacent Bedford Basin, passing by here as they set out for Britain.

Since the founding of Halifax in 1746, the reef-studded shorelines to the east and west have seen hundreds of wrecks. The first light on Chebucto Head was erected in 1872, more than a century after Sambro Island light. The modern, reinforced concrete tower dates from 1977. This station is readily accessible from Halifax via Purcell's Cove Road.

George's Island

Now officially described as "Halifax Harbour Inner Range", a lighthouse has stood sentinel on the shore of George's Island in Halifax Harbour since 1876. Today it is a 17m (55 ft.), octagonal tower, red-capped and bearing a fluorescent, red, vertical stripe on the seaward side. Nearby are old fortifications spanning a couple of centuries, including a colonial fortress, with wall and moat, and gun emplacements from both World Wars. The site is currently closed to the public, but Parks Canada plans to restore the old fort and make it accessible to the public. The light is visible from the seaward end of the Historic Properties on the Halifax waterfront.

HALIFAX
to **CANSO**

Maugher's Beach, Nova Scotia

Maugher's Beach

Maugher's Beach light station on the east side of the entrance to Halifax Harbour was one of the last glimpses of land for thousands of men sailing for Europe in both World Wars. At one time it was a complete station with keepers' houses, service buildings and dock. Now, on a rock-ballasted point, the tower stands alone.

The reinforced concrete octagonal tower is 14.6m (50 ft.) high. A flaring concrete platform supports an octagonal aluminum lamphouse with an automatic light. It is all that is left to remind us of a very long history dating back to 1814 when the military built a massive granite, martello tower on the end of the spit and mounted several defensive guns. When, in 1826, marine interests demanded that a light be built there, the Legislature of Nova Scotia had a beacon mounted on the existing stone tower in order to save money. The current concrete tower was built in 1941 to replace the old tower, but it was several years before the old stone martello tower and its foundations were removed. The foghorn was discontinued in 1993 after 104 years of sounding through the Atlantic fogs.

Spits and bars of the type at Maugher's Beach are, by definition, temporary structures subject to waves and currents so Maugher's Beach spit was rebuilt in 1987 and heavily ballasted with large rocks. The residence and other buildings were torn down at the same time.

In 1851, Abraham Gesner, a Nova Scotia physician and inventor, brought his new discovery, kerosene oil distilled from coal, to the lamps at Maugher's Beach. After an unimpressive start, the flame proved far brighter and easier to control, and was also much more economical than earlier fuels. It soon became the standard lighthouse fuel in Canada and in many other countries. Maugher's Beach light is accessible by a small ferry that crosses from Eastern Passage to McNabb's Island. From the landing there is a footpath to the site.

Sable Island

Sable Island lies in the open Atlantic a little more than 170 nautical miles east-southeast of Halifax. It is a 34-km-long (21-mi.) crescent-shaped deposit of sand and gravel left by the glaciers 12,000 years ago. Shallows and reefs extend for miles beyond each end of the island, creating a hazard to navigation since ships first came across the Atlantic. Lying astride the main shipping routes, it has claimed hundreds of ships which were soon swallowed by the drifting sands, perhaps to be exhumed again decades later as erosion patterns changed. Before radio, many vessels sailed out into the Eastern Atlantic and were never seen again, "lost with all hands". It is not known how many of them came to lonely grief on Sable Island.

Its lighthouse history dates back to the 18th century when concern grew about the number of ships lost there. By 1801, a modest life-saving station was placed on the island. These were the days when the argument still raged—would a lighthouse draw ships to their doom or warn them off? Finally, in 1873, lighthouses were built on each end of Sable Island.

Erosion on the west end of the sandy island was severe and massive Atlantic storms removed hundreds of metres of land from time to time. In the years until 1940, the west light was moved six times for a total distance of 16 kms (10 mi). On one occasion, the alarmed keepers removed valuable equipment just in time to watch the lighthouse foundations crumble into the waves. The east light has had a much more stable existence, and while the tower has been replaced several times, it remains on the original spot about eight kms (5 mi.) from the end of land. Both were square concrete towers with steel outer frames for stability. Their lights were visible for more than 20 kms (12 mi.).

Sable Island is perhaps most remarkable for its herd of wild horses. They have adapted and maintain themselves at about 250 head. These days, the Sable Island area is the scene of oil and gas exploration. The island is a restricted area.

Eddy Point

Northbound ships along the Atlantic coast wanting to head into the Gulf of St. Lawrence used to save many miles by cutting through Canso Strait, between Cape Breton Island and mainland Nova Scotia. Even after the construction of the causeway across the Strait, smaller ships still travel this route via the canal lock. A lighthouse was built in 1851 on the low sand and gravel spit on the south side of the Atlantic entrance to the Strait. This original tower was replaced with a second tower—square, with a square lanternhouse—and nearby keeper's residence. Around 1988, this second tower was replaced with a round steel tower with a plain octagonal lanternhouse, 8.6m (28 ft.) tall, and the remaining buildings were removed. The site is accessible from the Trans Canada Highway by turning south on NS 344 at Mulgrave for 14 kms (9 mi.) to Sand Point, where a local road, marked as Eddy Point Lighthouse, takes you to the tower beside the sea.

CAPE BRETON ISLAND

Cape North, Nova Scotia

Louisbourg

Prior to 1730, fires were lit to guide ships entering on the east side of Louisbourg (its French spelling) Harbour, the site of a French fortress. These fires did not prove very effective so, in 1731, Louis XV authorized a stone tower 20m (66 ft.) high to be built. Designed with a wooden light chamber on top, the light was provided by an open coal fire. The top was soon destroyed by fire and replaced with a masonry top and oil lamps. The tower lasted until 1758 when British artillery put it out of commission. It was not until 1842 that a new wooden lighthouse was built. This one lasted until the current octagonal reinforced concrete tower was installed in 1923. Its 1902 diaphone was replaced with electronic horns in 1972.

The magnificent, reconstructed fortress of Louisbourg is accessible by principal highways in Cape Breton. Old stones and bits of masonry around the lighthouse base reflect the site's long history.

Cape North

At least a million people a year pass by the red and white, checkerboard, Cape North tower and light... now in front of the National Museum of Science and Technology in Ottawa. Its 3rd Order Fresnel lens now throws its rotating beam out over the museum grounds and the traffic on St. Laurent Boulevard. As Director of the museum in 1978, I had wanted to display a real lighthouse beside the big steam locomotive, the Agena rocket, the large radar dish and the astronomy dome that were already on the grounds.

So when the Superintendent of Marine Aids, John Ballinger, called one day to say that the cast-iron tower at Cape North on the north tip of Cape Breton Island was to be replaced, a museum crew was immediately dispatched. At Cape North a few weeks later, a convoy of tractor trailers, loaded with the dismantled lighthouse, with bulldozers pushing from behind, struggled to climb the steep trail from the shoreline to the main road, 310m (1,000 ft.) above. Luckily they succeeded, for the very next day the rudimentary roadway was snowed in for the winter.

Once back at the museum workshops, a new reinforced concrete light platform had to be designed and built to replace the original, which had been eaten away by salt spray over the decades. The lamphouse had to be refurbished and painted, the lens and rotating gear cleaned and repaired, a solid new foundation provided on the grounds, and a dozen or so new stanchions for railings cast in a local foundry to match those on the light platform itself.

In the spring of 1979, the new base was ready and the two-ton plates were reassembled. The new concrete platform dangled on the end of a long boom to be lowered onto the tower. Then the lamphouse and finally the lenses and light were installed. The original checkerboard pattern of red and white squares was carefully reapplied. Huge limestone blocks, donated by a local quarry company, were carefully arranged to give the impression of a lighthouse on an island, albeit in a sea of grass.

Groups of school children and other visitors can now troop through a real lighthouse in conducted tours. Thousands of passers-by see its rotating Fresnel lens flashing atop its red and white tower every day. Its original location is accessible for the hardy who are willing to walk down the steep, rough road from the high plateau to the shore. Today they will find a very modest, automated light on a plain, wooden tower.

Cellar below the lamphouse being installed

Hoisted lamphouse

Lamphouse on its way to the top of the tower

St. Paul's Island

St. Paul's Island (North)

It was a fine summer's day, with calm seas and gentle breezes when the helicopter set me down on St. Paul's Island. In the distance the horizon was sharp and flat with the northern tip of Cape Breton just visible 25 kms (16 mi.) to the southwest. As I took in the tranquil scene, I tried to visualize the place as T.H. Tidmarsh, a Nova Scotia lighthouse commissioner, had described it on a visit in 1833,

> ...our route gave us a melancholy view of the numerous wrecks with which the shore is strewed, the whole coast is covered with pieces of the wreck of ships and in some places there is an accumulation of shipwreck nearly sufficient to rebuild smaller ones... The number of graves bore strong testimony also that some guide or land mark was wanting in the quarter to guard and direct the approach of strangers to this boisterous, rugged shore. (after Bush, p. 39)

Replacement tower 1916

The history of Cape Breton's northern tip was full of tragedy. In 1833, ten ships were lost on the outer shores of Cape Breton Island with 603 lives lost. In 1834, *Astrea* crashed ashore with 240 lost. When *Sibylle* with 316 aboard sank off St. Paul's with all hands there was a public uproar. Some of *Jessie's* 27 passengers and crew struggled ashore after foundering there, and died weeks later of cold and starvation. After more years of debate about who would finance a lighthouse, a joint agreement was struck among the British Admiralty, Canada, Nova Scotia, New Brunswick and little P.E.I. Two lights were finally underway, one at each end of St. Paul's Island. They were completed in 1839.

The original lighthouses were 12.5m (40 ft.), tapering, octagonal, wooden buildings and equipped with polygonal iron lanterns with flat glass panes. In 1914, the south end light was completely destroyed by fire. It was replaced in 1916 by a stumpy, round, cast-iron tower only 4m (12 ft.) high, carrying a 3m (10 ft.) polygonal lamphouse with a flashing, petroleum vapour lamp. It is not a

graceful figure but it is still there after 80 years. On the north end, the original light tower was replaced in 1962 by a standard reinforced concrete tower 14.6m (47 ft.) high.

Now St. Paul's is automated and unstaffed, and shipwrecks are virtually unheard of. Turning on the fog horn is no longer a matter of the keeper's gut feeling or his having spied a thick, white bank rolling in—the radar sensor says it is time. The only human voices are those of the technicians on their infrequent maintainence visits. After the helicopter leaves, the only sounds are the cries of wheeling gulls and the distant surge of the surf.

Panmure, P.E.I.

PRINCE EDWARD ISLAND

Long known as the "garden of the gulf", Prince Edward Island is famous for its lush green fields, and its thousands of acres of potatoes and general farmland. Prince Edward Island also has a unique place in Canada's lighthouse history. The north side of its crescent shape faces the Gulf of St. Lawrence. The south side is a series of low cliffs of red sandstone and shale alternating with long beaches and bars of reddish sands, facing the warm, sheltered waters of Northumberland Strait. For centuries, fleets of fishermen have sailed out onto the seas from sheltered places along the coast.

All of these refuges have been marked with local harbour lights, range lights and channel markers. Several major lights were also built in the 19th century to aid shipping in the Gulf, notably at East Point and North Point. Other lights were built for the Northumberland Strait from Souris in the east to West Point. Most of the lights are superbly constructed and well-maintained wooden structures, long a matter of pride for Islanders. This is probably the only place in Canada where lighthouses can be seen in the middle of potato fields.

Range lights are aids for entering bays, inlets and harbours and normally consist of an outer light on a point, island or shoal, and an inner or back light, usually much higher and set in from shore. These markers are useful in small harbours and channels in daylight, but are especially needed at night when their lights are lined up to allow entry with confidence. Prince Edward Island has several, interesting range lights, with some of the back lights famous for their tall, skinny, even awkward, shapes (see photo p.103).

Lighthouses are a celebrated part of Prince Edward Island's tourism. As the stations have been automated and destaffed, many have been adopted by societies of local citizens. Their activities range from care and preservation, to operating museums, to running a bed and breakfast, such as at West Point.

PRINCE EDWARD ISLAND

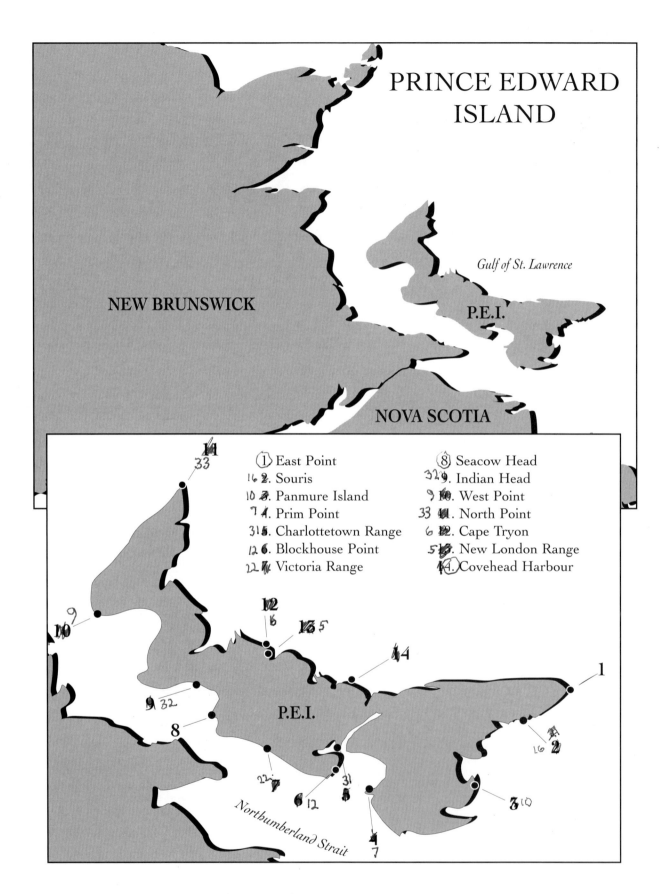

Gulf of St. Lawrence

NEW BRUNSWICK

P.E.I.

NOVA SCOTIA

1. East Point
2. Souris
3. Panmure Island
4. Prim Point
5. Charlottetown Range
6. Blockhouse Point
7. Victoria Range
8. Seacow Head
9. Indian Head
10. West Point
11. North Point
12. Cape Tryon
13. New London Range
14. Covehead Harbour

P.E.I.

Northumberland Strait

NORTHUMBERLAND STRAIT

Summerside Back Range, P.E.I.

East Point

The first lighthouse at East Point on Prince Edward Island was built in 1867 on the eastern tip of the island about half a mile from the end of the point. When H.M.S. *Phoenix* sank on a nearby offshore reef in 1882, the distance of the lighthouse from the point—and therefore from the hazards—was partially blamed. The whole structure was moved much closer to the dangerous shore. Only 25 years later, erosion threatened the tower, so it was moved again, 200 feet to its current position. Having survived two moves, the tower is solid testimony to the builders' construction practices. Eroding cliffs and retreating lights have long been part of the Island scene. Most recently, Cape Egmont light was moved back from the cliff front in 1998.

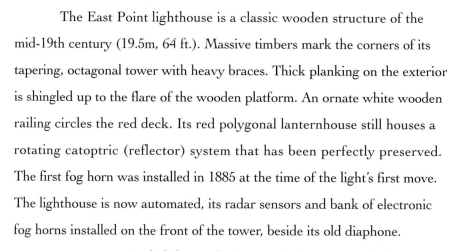

The East Point lighthouse is a classic wooden structure of the mid-19th century (19.5m, 64 ft.). Massive timbers mark the corners of its tapering, octagonal tower with heavy braces. Thick planking on the exterior is shingled up to the flare of the wooden platform. An ornate white wooden railing circles the red deck. Its red polygonal lanternhouse still houses a rotating catoptric (reflector) system that has been perfectly preserved. The first fog horn was installed in 1885 at the time of the light's first move. The lighthouse is now automated, its radar sensors and bank of electronic fog horns installed on the front of the tower, beside its old diaphone.

Its lighthouse duties completely automated, the station is now preserved and operated as a tourist attraction by a local group. It is accessible by a side road leading northeast from the main coastal Route 16 at the east end of Prince Edward Island.

Souris

A square, tapering 14.3m (47 ft.) tower has a square platform supported by scrolled, wooden brackets. It is topped by a severe, round, red lanternhouse with a ventilation cap. It formerly housed a rotating Fresnel lens (see photo). Long ago automated, it runs on mainland power, and has a bull's-eye type light and a bank of electronic horns. The light marks the entrance to Souris Harbour for the Magdalen Islands' ferry and for coastal boats along the eastern end of P.E.I. It can be reached by taking a small sideroad off coastal Route 16.

Panmure Island

PEI - 10

Panmure Island, on the east side of Prince Edward Island, is linked to the mainland by a long bar, now a Provincial Park. It marks the south side of Georgetown Harbour and bears a major lighthouse on its outer edge. Along with East Point and West Point, this is one of Prince Edward Island's large and handsome wooden towers.

Its massive, tapering, octagonal tower is capped with a matching octagonal platform on scrolled, wooden, supporting brackets. Neatly-framed windows mark each of the four interior levels. Built in 1853, its rotating lens system is in one of the large polygonal lamphouses typical of light-houses when oil lamps required a lot of surrounding space. On the apex of the tower is a large vent, further evidence of former fuel-burning days. Supporting rods lead from the railing stanchions to the edge of the roof. Lantern windows are especially tall rectangles of plain glass. Inside, the main frame is made up of massive, hand-hewn timbers.

Panmure Island lighthouse is a "must see". It is accessible from Montague on Route 17, then Route 347 through Panmure Island Provincial Park.

Prim Point

Built in 1846, Prim Point is P.E.I.'s oldest lighthouse, and arguably its most beautiful. It stands on a long point on the southeast side of Hillsborough Bay, on the outer approaches to Charlottetown Harbour on Northumberland Strait. Its tapering, round tower is capped by a multi-sided platform supported by graceful brackets. Its ten-sided, red lanternhouse, with tall, rectangular, glass panes is capped by a wind-directed vent and has supporting rods from roofline to railing stanchions. The central core of the tower is brick, sheathed in wood and shingled in an unusually fine display of that art.

Inside, four flights of stairs with four landings and inset windows lead to the lantern level. An electric motor hums away, rotating the original Fresnel lens system. Remnants of the original clockwork mechanism stand by, reminders of the days when keepers climbed to the top every few hours to crank the heavy weights.

Still largely in its original condition with its Fresnel lens, Prim Point was completely automated by 1976. Today it stands alone on its commanding site overlooking the red P.E.I. shoreline below. It is accessible on local roads leading out of the east side of Charlottetown.

Charlottetown Range PEL-31

This unusual, hexagonal tower is part of the range light system in Charlottetown Harbour. It is listed officially as the Brighton Beach Range and since this photograph was taken, its daymark has been altered from horizontal red bands to a vertical red stripe. A similar Coast Guard tower design is found in a few other places such as False Ducks in Lake Ontario and Point Escuminac in New Brunswick. This one is unique, however, in that the light peers out from under the platform instead of being mounted on top.

Blockhouse Point

PEI - 12

Prince Edward Island has many examples of beautifully-built, wooden lighthouses. But outstanding for fine craftsmanship, even among these, is Blockhouse Point. It is a combined residence and tower with superbly crafted windows, doors, and cornices including around the base of the platform. The light tower is square, 12.2m (41 ft.) high with an octagonal lanternhouse and an omnidirectional lens. Its electric light gives a three second flash with a one second eclipse, more a wink than a flash. It is accessible from the coastal road, Route 19, on the west side of the entrance to Charlottetown Harbour. See p. 33 as well.

Victoria Harbour Range PEI-22

Route 1 crosses Victoria Harbour on the south side of Prince Edward Island about halfway between Charlottetown and Summerside with the range lights visible from the bridge. This backlight (1878) is a standard, tapering, square tower with square, wooden platform, octagonal lamphouse and wind-controlled vent on top. Its daymark is a bright red diamond on its white front.

Seacow Head

PEI-B

Seacow Head on the extreme southeast side of the entrance to Bedeque Bay and Summerside Harbour, is part of a series of lights along the Northumberland Strait side of Prince Edward Island. Built in 1863, its 18.3m (60 ft.) octagonal wooden tower is another of the classic P.E.I. towers. Tapering, with white shingles, it has a platform with red railing which supports a red, polygonal lantern with tall, flat, glass panes. Inside, its heavy timbers are visible with three iron rods across each of its three levels serving as braces. Its imported stone foundations are set on the soft, red island rocks below ground level. Seacow Head can be reached from Route 119 and via roads leading southwest from Central Bedeque, east of Summerside on Route 1A.

Indian Head

A casual glance out the harbour from the main road into Summerside from Borden is rewarded by a glimpse of a small white finger on the end of a bar on the south side of the bay. This lighthouse is accessible by taking P.E.I. 171 west from Bedeque. Turn right onto 121 and keep going past the pavement, past the gravel and a short distance along a red dirt road to emerge on a grassy point with a beautiful view of sea and coast. Great blocks of khaki sandstone from Wallace, N.S. make a breakwater half a kilometre long. On its end a 32-sided lighthouse: an octagonal, concrete base rising from the mud, topped by an octagonal main house, then an octagonal tower leading to an octagonal lamphouse.

It was nearly high tide when I arrived one late summer afternoon in 1998. A few swimmers were enjoying the warm salt water that splashed through low spots in the breakwater. They counselled that we could walk out to the light at low tide, which would come just after noon the next day. Sure enough, when I returned the next day, it was an easy walk, to the light. Built in 1881, the light is now automated. Its omnidirectional Fresnel lens provides a five-second electric flash followed by a five second eclipse. It is an odd, little gem and is located in an accessible and picturesque spot.

West Point `PEI-9`

West Point is aptly named for it is where the Northumberland Strait shoreline of Prince Edward Island turns from east—west to south—north towards North Point, the very end of the Island. The light-house is a classical wooden P.E.I. tower although it is square in cross section rather than the more standard octagonal shape. Straight flights of stairs rise up three levels to the platform and its original 12—sided, cast-iron lamphouse, perched 20m (65 ft.) above the ground.

Tourist literature often features the West Point light because of its bold daymark: three broad, black, horizontal stripes across its white tower. Multiple black, horizontal stripes are uncommon in Canadian lights. Race Rocks, B.C. is the only one of similar appearance.

When automation and destaffing left the light abandoned, a local community group moved in, built an addition to replace the old demolished dwelling and, in 1988, converted this historic light station into an inn and restaurant. Local lore would have it that Captain Kidd buried some of his treasure in the sand dunes north of the light. Visitors in the tower are urged to watch offshore for a mysterious, burning, ghost ship.

To get to West Point, take Route 2 to Carleton, then coastal Route 12 along a very short side road to the lighthouse and Cedar Dunes Provincial Park.

GULF *of* ST. LAWRENCE COAST

PEI - 33

North Point, P.E.I.

North Point PEI- 33

Standing alone in a grassy, field just back of the northwest tip of P.E.I., is a superb wooden lighthouse, built in 1866 in the best tradition of the Island. North Point is a principal warning light in the western Gulf of St. Lawrence. Erosion has caused the lighthouse to be moved back from the point several times.

Its smoothly tapering, octagonal, shingled walls lead to a platform circled by ornate wooden railing. It has a 12-sided red lamphouse and dome with a wind-directed ventilation funnel. A dioptric lens system with electric light was installed in 1970, creating a beacon visible about 15 nautical miles out to sea.

North Point can be reached by travelling west on Route 2, then north to Tignish, and to the end of Route 12, the shore road.

Cape Tryon PEI- 6

Built in 1976 to replace its 1905 predecessor, a 12m (40 ft.) tower now sits on Cape Tryon on the north coast of Prince Edward Island, north-northeast of Summerside. It is a beautifully-crafted, square, wooden tower with a square platform and lamphouse with simple, rectangular, glass panes. The light flashes for two seconds then eclipses for four. It is accessible by a short side road from Route 20 using the power line as a guide.

New London Range PGT- 5

For the lighthouse "collector", the range lights on the northwest side of New London Bay (on the north shore of Prince Edward Island) are especially attractive. The front range light is a routine square steel tower on wooden piles set in the reddish sand beach, with a bright red diamond on its rectangular, white lattice front. The back light is the real attraction. It is a tapering square tower with a small, red-roofed house attached to the rear. As the tower tapers upward, it changes to a straight, four-square shape on past its lightly built platform, to a square unadorned top bearing a hexagonal lanternhouse with simple square glass panes (see photo).

Set in the grass among the red beaches and dunes, its simple, white tower with small house make a charming sight. It is accessible by a short side road from the coastal Route 6, in the middle of the north side of Prince Edward Island. With the nearby Cape Tryon light, the New London Range is a lighthouse destination of note.

Covehead Harbour

By adding an unusual bracket system under the platform, the carpenter who built this 8.2m (27 ft.) tower distinguished it from the crowd of small wooden lighthouses, so characteristic of Prince Edward Island. Its feet are firmly planted in the sand at the west end of Stanhope Beach in Prince Edward Island National Park. The park is at the entrance to Covehead Harbour directly north of Charlottetown. Its lanternhouse is a square-windowed structure, blinded on the landward side. It is operated on a seasonal basis.

Head Harbour, New Brunswick

NEW BRUNSWICK

In terms of coastlines, New Brunswick has two types. The first is the rocky, rugged, tide-washed Bay of Fundy to the south. The second is the much gentler eastern shore running from the Nova Scotia boundary to the head of Bay Chaleur and composed of sandy shorelines and long offshore bars. Navigation and shipping along these shores have had a unique past.

The New Brunswick shore of the Bay of Fundy forms one side of the main shipping route into the province's major port of Saint John. When loyalist settlers flooded the region in the late 1700s, navigation aids were desperately needed to guide small sailing ships through deadly tidal currents and dense fog. With few harbours or inlets to provide shelter, marine disasters were common. Not surprisingly, major lights were constructed early with Seal Island in 1830; Nova Scotia's Brier Island at the southern entrance to the Bay of Fundy in 1809; Partridge Island at the harbour mouth of Saint John (as early as 1790); Gannet Rock (1831) and Grand Manan, (1860).

The eastern shore of New Brunswick has a very different history. Shore fisheries—lobster and herring—were operated from small villages all the way up to the Miramichi. The waters were often treacherous with sandy shoals and shifting bars endangering passing fishing boats and lumber ships. The region's lighthouses provided guidance to fleets of fishing vessels returning home with their daily catch to places like Miscou or Shippegan. These places were served by local lights, range lights, spars and buoys but had none of the great landfall lights such as those at the entrance to the Bay of Fundy.

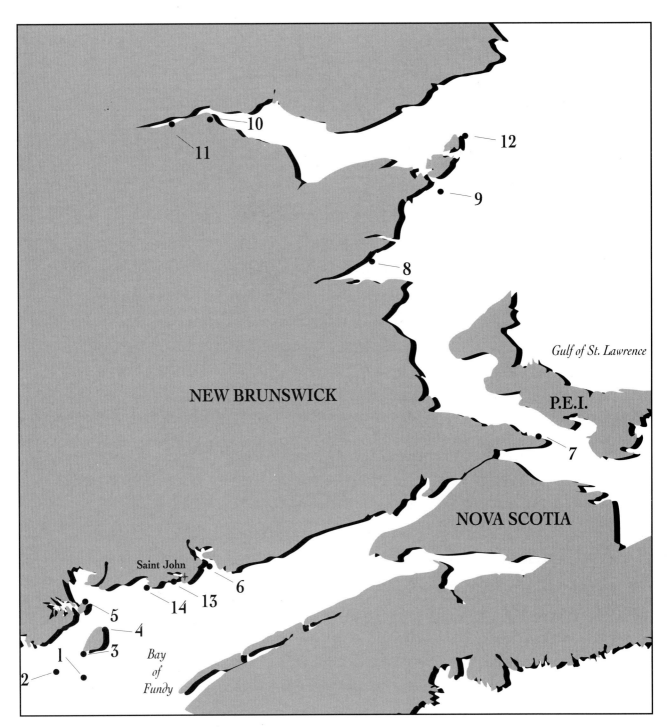

NEW BRUNSWICK

1. Gannet Rock NB-6
2. Machias Seal Island NB-7
3. Southwest Head
4. Swallowtail NB-1
5. Head Harbour NB-3

6. Partridge Island NB-21
7. Cape Jourimain NB-22
8. Grand Dune Range NB-23
9. Big Shippigan NB-24
10. Inch Arran NB-25

11. Campbellton NB-26
12. Miscou NB-16 NB-19
13. Musquash NB-20

Gannet Rock, New Brunswick

BAY *of* FUNDY COAST

Musquash Point, New Brunswick

Gannet Rock

About the closest Canada has to a major lighthouse on a wave-washed rock is at Gannet Rock, 10kms (6 mi.) southwest of Grand Manan, New Brunswick, at the entrance to the Bay of Fundy. At high tide, a very small rocky island of a few square metres is all that shows above water. In stormy weather, it is all wave-washed. When a sturdy, wooden, octagonal tower of massive, hand-hewn timbers was erected on a stone base in 1831, many prophesied imminent doom. After the lighthouse survived a wild gale in the winter of 1842, authorities added a retaining wall that was later jacketed in cement.

Now fully automated, gannet Rock stands alone in the sea, its diesel generators supplying power to its two-lensed airport-type beacon. The beacon shines from an octagonal, aluminum lamphouse, installed in 1967. It will soon be converted to solar-generated electricity following the pattern of most east coast lights. It is interesting to look up at the old light with its tapering black and white daymark and wire braces and realize that the lighthouse's gloomy critics of the 1830s have been dead for more than a century. Gannet Rock is not accessible except by boat in fine weather and landing is discouraged.

Machias Seal Island

NB-7

In 1832, a wooden lighthouse was erected on a low, uninhabited rocky island in international waters, 11 nautical miles southwest of Grand Manan and 12 nautical miles off the coast of Maine. It was a little shorter but in most respects similar to the one still serving on nearby Gannet Rock. Parabolic reflectors with individual lamps supplied the first light but these were soon replaced by a more effective arrangement with a single multi-wick Argand lamp. The current reinforced-concrete tower dates from 1915. Today, the beacon is a large rotating, double-ended bull's eye searchlight. The power is generated in an extremely noisy engine room at the base of the tower (see p.27).

The site is home to some interesting wildlife. At the south end of the Grand Manan, at the mouth of the Bay of Fundy, the sea is full of fish attracted by cold, nutrient-rich waters churned up by the tidal currents. In turn, whales and seabirds are attracted by the abundant fish. Machias Seal is a nesting place for terns, gannets and guillemots and is now a protected wildlife sanctuary. Carefully scheduled and supervised trips are available for bird watchers leaving from both Maine and Grand Manan, N.B.

In the early 1980s, a debate flared up between Canada and the United States over ownership of the Island. Nations around the world had recently expanded their coastal boundaries to 200 nautical miles, and the rich fishing grounds around Machias Seal were now under dispute. Canada argued that its lightkeepers had occupied the island for 150 years and that traditional international boundary customs of drawing borders halfway between two countries clearly placed the territory in Canadian waters. In 1984, an international court at the Hague agreed and today's maps now show the island inside the Canadian border.

Machias Seal is not accessible except by charter boat and restrictions apply to landing because it is a sanctuary.

Puffins at Machias Seal

Southwest Head

Perched on the edge of the cliffs at the southwest end of Grand Manan Island, Southwest Head light station was once part of a spectacular scene. A victim of automation, today only a short, square tower, radio tower and small service building remain. Nonetheless, the tower still sends its beacon light out over the cliffs and jagged rocks below, alerting mariners in the approaches to the Bay of Fundy. On clear days the American coast is visible to the northwest, while to the southwest, Gannet Rock and Machias Seal Island lighthouses appear as small dots in the sea.

Southwest Head is readily accessible by following the main road on Grand Manan, Route 776, southward until it ends at the light station parking lot. Visitors are treated to marvelous seascapes and an ocean full of marine life, including whales, dolphins and sea birds.

Swallowtail

NB-2

Grand Manan Island lies in the Bay of Fundy at the extreme southwest corner of New Brunswick at the boundary between Canada and the United States. It is a Mecca for whale and bird watchers and those wanting to enjoy marine scenery and a quiet pace of life. Swallowtail lighthouse is perched on the rocky point on the north side of North Head Harbour where the ferry lands. Erected in 1860, its white, octagonal tower (16.2m (53 ft.) is braced by cables extending from anchors in the rock to just below the platform. Oddly enough, the platform only has seven sides. The red, octagonal lamphouse houses a rotating beacon. On nights without fog, I have seen its flash clearly from my brother's house in Pocologan on the New Brunswick shore some 40kms (25 mi.) away.

The lighthouse is easily accessible from North Head ferry landing, the last half mile or so on foot. When I visited in 1980, I enjoyed a delicious, fresh fish chowder ("fish" = "cod" in local parlance) with the keeper and his family. Now the keeper's house is a tea room and Bed and Breakfast.

Head Harbour

NB-3

Among the several hundred lighthouses in Canada, the most famous tourist sites—appearing in calendars, tourist literature and pictorial books—are Peggy's Point on its wave-washed granite point in Nova Scotia, and Head Harbour on Campobello Island, New Brunswick. Head Harbour is famous for its prominent red, St. George's Cross "daymark" on its white tower.

Several other lights near Head Harbour have distinctive daymarks, most notably the nearby West Quoddy Head in Maine. With its eight red and seven white stripes, it is a regular barber pole. Daymarks help mariners see towers against white hillsides, fog banks or through mist and drizzle.

Campobello Island is accessible by causeway from Lubec, Maine, and from southern New Brunswick by ferry via Deer Island. Roads and footpaths lead to the Head Harbour light station on the northern tip of the island.

Partridge Island

Partridge Island is a high, rocky island at the entrance to Saint John Harbour and the mouth of the St. John River. During the later days of the American revolution and the years following, shiploads of Loyalists came in to Saint John, spreading out over southern New Brunswick and up the river into the interior. By 1791, a lighthouse had been placed on Partridge Island but little is known of its subsequent history and ultimate demise. The existing 13.8m (46 ft.) octagonal, concrete tower dates from 1961 and is now entirely automated with an airport-type beacon light. Brilliant red sides alternate with white ones on its octagonal flanks to make a highly visible daymark in the especially foggy place. My first visit to a lighthouse was to an earlier tower at this site in 1932, when I was shown the Fresnel lens and its clockwork mechanism with a mercury "float" by keeper Lauder and his son.

Sadly, the fog horn was discontinued in 1998. In 1860, Partridge Island was the scene of the first steam fog whistle with a clockwork mechanism to keep its signal regular in frequency and duration. In 1902, J.P. Northey of Toronto developed the diaphone horn wherein a horizontally pulsing piston produced a low note that carried over the sea for many miles. This Canadian invention spread rapidly all over the world. By 1904, Partridge Island had a diaphone of its own. I recall fondly that all through my own boyhood in this foggy city I used to hear the Partridge Island "groaner" sending out its booming signal on foggy nights. In later years, this was changed to a two-tone signal with a long low note followed without interruption by a shorter, even lower note. Frequencies were chosen to maximize how far the horn could be heard.

Now Partridge Island sends out its light beams in silence. The keepers' houses are boarded up. The immigration and quarantine hospitals have mostly been demolished. Graveyards among the bushes, and fortifications from past wars are weathering away. A large Celtic cross stands on the island, a reminder of the hundreds of immigrants who died here in the 18th and early 19th centuries.

Partridge Island is only accessible by boat or helicopter. It can be seen from the Digby ferry or with binoculars from Fort Dufferin and the end of City Line (a street in West Saint John). Its history and proximity to a major city makes the lighthouse an ideal candidate for a National Historic Site and public park.

EAST COAST *to* CHALEUR BAY

NB-19

Miscou Island, New Brunswick

Cape Jourimain

A lovely old wooden lighthouse stands on low ground just east of the New Brunswick end of the Confederation Bridge to P.E.I. Once visible to passengers on the old ferries that operated from nearby Cape Tormentine, it can now be seen from the approaches and southwestern end of the bridge. The bridge has made a lighthouse largely redundant. The area around it is now a wildlife refuge. There are future plans for public access and to develop the old lighthouse as an information centre.

The octagonal, wooden tower tapers upward to a collar of nicely finished wood-work, looking like an old lantern platform. From here the tower rises another 3m (10 ft.) to the real platform with its plain wooden balustrade and fancy scrolled supports. A ten-sided lantern house with flat, square panes is capped with a mushroom-shaped vent for its original oil lamps. Note the swallows' nests under the light platform.

Cape Jourimain light is accessible with some effort from the service road alongside the west or New Brunswick end of the bridge with footpaths beyond. If present plans hold, the ecological reserve will become open to the public.

Grand Dune Range NB-23

Grand Dune caisson under construction

Low, sandy islands, spits and shoals mark the entrance to Miramichi Bay on the east coast of New Brunswick. One of several range lights in the area is called Grand Dune. It is a caisson type surrounded by water. The cylindrical iron base is filled with stone and gravel and displays a small pole light and a white daymark, with a red, vertical stripe on the seaward side.

Big Shippegan NB-24

An octagonal, wooden tower with red lamphouse was placed on a sand bar on the east side of Shippegan "Gully" (meaning "harbour entry") in 1872. Its neat, tapering shingled sides lead upward in a well-crafted flare to its wooden platform and red railing. Its round lamphouse with red roof and curved glass panes, spherical cap and weather vane are typical of the tops manufactured by Bernier. The tower's base is unusual in that the shingled sides end about a metre above ground, revealing concrete posts which are set in the sand on each corner and in the centre.

The lighthouse is accessible along a local road out of the town of Shippegan, which exits the main Route 11 between Pokemouche and Haut Pokemouche.

Inch Arran NB-25

A unique lighthouse building stands at the eastern end of Victoria Street next to a city park in Dalhousie, New Brunswick. A tapering, square, wooden tower 10.9m (34 ft.) high holds an octagonal lamphouse from which a set of thin railings stretches out like a bird cage all the way up to the gutter edges of the dome. This odd feature is to prevent gulls from nesting there. The clearly visible lens is a 2nd Order fixed catoptric with an electric light flashing every few seconds, forming the front of the range. The back marker with red stripe daymark is visible through the trees to the west.

The main tower is primarily white, with all of its features—door, windows, edges of the tower, railings, and platform supports—picked in Coast Guard red and decorative maple leaves.

Campbellton NB-26

Along the waterfront in Campbellton on the shore of Bay Chaleur, one will find a beautifully maintained residence and light tower, enclosed in a white fence with neat grounds. It is officially called the Campbellton Rear Range and was a simple steel tower until recently, when the Town of Campbellton built a 15.2m (53 ft.) tower around it and a residence beside it. The residence operates as a hostel. The new tower is a tapering octagon with a somewhat flattened lanternhouse and a red stripe on the seaward side. It is a splendid example of how an otherwise undistinguished range light was transformed into a town landmark.

QC-16

Southwest Point, Anticosti, Quebec

QUEBEC

The Province of Quebec has a variety of coastlines: from the estuarine St. Lawrence below Quebec City to the rugged, glaciated, Precambrian Shield rocks along the north shore. Low shorelines mark the flat-lying limestones of Anticosti Island, and red sandstone and cliffs of shale the Magdalens, a group of islands connected by long sand bars. The lighthouse history in Quebec is also diverse and is connected with the history of settlement along the coasts and farther inland.

The English and the French had largely resolved their wars over Canada by 1770 and settlement to the west of the mouth of the St. Lawrence began in earnest. Having survived the Atlantic crossing and the marine hazards of Newfoundland and Nova Scotia, ships (many loaded with immigrants) went upriver past the Gaspé and Anticosti, only to encounter the sandbars, islands and shifting currents of the St. Lawrence. By 1800, multiple wrecks made it painfully clear that lighthouses were needed badly. In 1809, the first light was erected on Green Island (Isle Verte) where it remains, the third oldest surviving lighthouse in Canada. On November 1 that year, the steam paddle wheeler *Accommodation* set out from Montreal on her maiden voyage. With no lights to guide her, travel was by daylight alone. The voyage to Quebec City took 66 hours. Today it would take a single day.

Naval ships, often on survey missions, were common along the coasts in those days. In their reports, captains regularly commented on the desperate need for lighthouses. In 1831, a light was built on Southwest Point on Anticosti Island. It was followed, in 1832, by another one on Pointe des Monts, on the north side of the River, considered by some to be where the sea begins. Constructed next were Heath Point on the east end of Anticosti in 1835, and Stone Pillar, not far below Quebec City, in 1843. Isle Bicquette, on the south shore below Green Island, followed in 1844; and Red Islet's massive stone tower, off the mouth of the Saguenay, in 1848. While these few lights were helpful, they were also reminders of how pitifully inadequate the lighthouse system was. Despite the apparent size of the estuary, navigable channels run between long sandbar areas and numerous islands, making navigation hazardous.

By 1850, shipowner Hugh Allen began to lose steamships along the St. Lawrence in his regular service from European ports to Montreal. When his *Canadian* was lost below Quebec City in 1857, his pleas - boosted by many Navy reports - were finally heard. Several light stations were established in 1858: at Belle Isle (S), West Point on Anticosti Island, and Cap des Rosiers on the end of the Gaspé Peninsula. Father Point (Point au Père) was lit in 1859 and later became the principal pilot station for the St. Lawrence.

After these initial bursts of construction, lighthouse progress was slow but steady. By World War I, the St. Lawrence was generally regarded as a well-marked waterway. Accidents happened from time to time but were mainly attributed to pilot error, as in the 1911 sinking of *Empress of Ireland*, just below Rimouski, with hundreds of lives lost.

Although fishing villages with their small vessels were a feature of Quebec's shores, it was the needs of the heavy ocean traffic into the heart of Canada that dominated Quebec's lighthouse history. Since the St. Lawrence Seaway opened in 1956, the St. Lawrence has also become the entrance to the heart of North America. Sept Isles on the north shore has become a principal shipping port for iron ore into the Great Lakes and out to world ports. Sailing ships once waited for daylight before they risked tacking back and forth as they beat up river. Now grain ships, tankers and container ships easily traverse these waters.

Ships today have radar, satellite position indictors, and even traffic control stations to guide them. Captains no longer need to fix on flashing lights and tall white towers. All lights in the Quebec region are automated. Replaced by steel skeleton towers, some of the original buildings have been abandoned, but many of them are being lovingly restored and preserved by local groups, proud of their lighthouses.

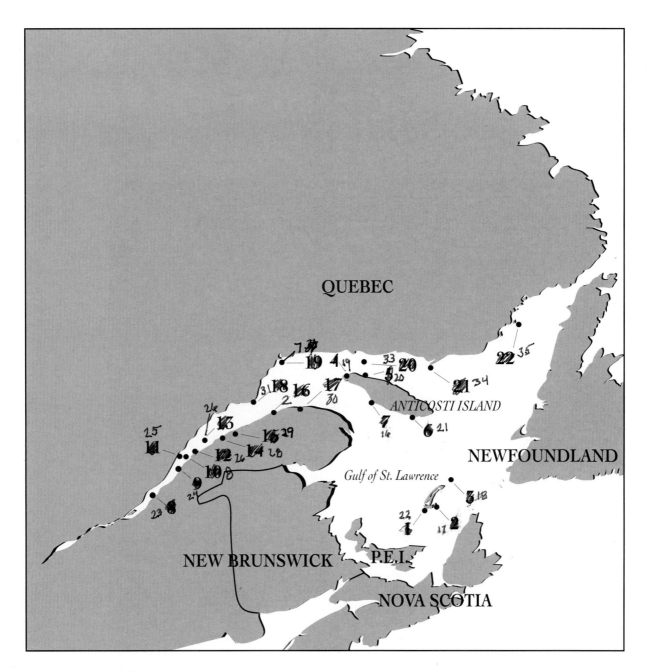

QUEBEC

MAGDALEN
ISLANDS

Bird Rocks, Quebec

QC-9

Magdalen Islands

Standing well out in the Gulf of St. Lawrence, the Magdalen Islands witnessed scores of shipwrecks in the first half of the 19th century. In the next several decades, thirty to forty vessels came to grief there. Not only were there mile-long sand bars joining these islands astride the shipping lanes, but the bars were also impossible to see during a storm amid the welter of breaking waves and blowing spume. Many unsuspecting vessels navigating by dead reckoning drove full tilt into the shifting sands, and were soon swallowed up. By 1875, five lighthouses had been built. Since then, other aids to navigation have been added from time to time. The present day Magdalen Islands are the centre of a substantial fishing industry. There is a salt mine deep under one of the islands. They are served by car ferry from Souris, Prince Edward Island and by airlines from the mainland.

Amherst Island

A light was first placed on this point of Amherst Island in 1871. This 1960s photograph of its successor shows its white hexagonal tower and rotating Fresnel lens system above the red cliffs. Bathers enjoy the shallow, warm, salt water below the old light, which was long ago modernized and automated.

Entry Island

Entry Island, part of the Magdalens (but not connected by sand bars), had its own lighthouse by 1874. Its successor, an automated, octagonal concrete tower, continues to send out a beacon light from its severe-looking 1960s lamphouse. Entry Island was settled primarily by English-speaking families, and the dominance of the language has continued with their descendants.

Bird Rocks

A group of small islands, ledges and shoals lies about 25 kms (16 mi.) northeast of the main group of the Magdalens. It is in an especially dangerous position, directly astride the main shipping route from the Atlantic Ocean through Cabot Strait and into the St. Lawrence River system. The largest of these is Great Bird Rock, an erosional remnant with receding cliffs of soft, red sandstone and conglomerate averaging 30m (100 ft.) high and rising mostly sheer from the wave line. Scattered along the cliffs are ledges, nooks and crannies that make ideal, summer nesting sites for thousands of gannets and other sea birds.

In his monumental 1830s survey of the Gulf of St. Lawrence, Captain Bayfield of the British Admiralty described Great Bird Rock as a very difficult place. When surveyors came in the 1860s before building a lighthouse, they could only find one or two ways up the perimeter cliffs to the flat, grassy top. They selected the least exposed indentation and built a small pier and ramp up an adjacent gully. Even so, Bird Rock could only be serviced in the calmest weather, usually in short periods in July and August. The station was complete by 1870. It had a 16m (50 ft.) wooden tower similar to those on Gannet and Machias Seal on the Bay of Fundy. It was equipped with a 2nd Order, Bernier-made, Fresnel lens.

Since then, the usual evolution through various oil lamps led to electricity in the 1960s. The original wooden structure was replaced by a hexagonal tower. It has a solid, concrete bottom half, and a shingled, wooden top supporting a red, octagonal lamphouse of the plain, contemporary design. In the early 1980s, it was still kept by two keepers who were helicoptered in for two-week shifts, and who alternated with another two-man crew. The station is no longer staffed and is highly inaccessible.

Gannets on Bird Rock

Shore of Bird Rock with gannets

ANTICOSTI ISLAND

Old Ellis Bay Range, Quebec

Anticosti Island

Anticosti Island, 215 kms (135 mi.) long and 48 kms (30 mi.) wide, raises its limestone cliffs, wooded hills and offshore shoals like a giant cork at the mouth of the St. Lawrence estuary. Main shipping routes pass on both the north and south sides and it has long been the place of shipwreck and tragedy. As early as 1827, Commander Bayfield realized that Anticosti should be marked at both ends. In addition, he advised that lights be erected at the tip of the Gaspé to the south, and at Pointe des Monts on the north shore.

After several years of arguing, principally over who should pay for these lights, a major station was established at Southwest Point about halfway along the south coast of Anticosti in 1831. In 1835 a second lighthouse went up on Heath Point on the east end of the island, and in 1858 a third on the west end. Others were added from time to time: Bagot Bluff in 1871, and on the north side, at Table Head, Carleton Point and Cap de Rabast, all in 1919.

West Point QC-19

The closest light station to Port Menier, the principal village and port on Anticosti, is West Point, at the westernmost extremity of the island. In 1858 a magnificent tower 33m (109 ft.) high and slightly tapering from its 12-m (40-ft.) diameter base, was erected on West Point overlooking extensive tidal flats. It was built of local limestone, faced with imported firebrick and it bore a round, decked lantern house.

Inside was a rotating Fresnel lens system of the 2nd Order. A similar tower can still be seen at Point Amour, on the Labrador coast of the Strait of Belle Isle near the Quebec border. In many respects these two resembled the famous Imperial towers of Lake Huron. They were all built about the same time by the Department of Public Works.

In 1967, after more than a century of service, the grand tower at West Point was replaced with a steel skeleton tower and airport beacon, and the old station was demolished. By the 1970s, a heap of limestone and firebrick rubble was all that remained of the once superb lighthouse.

Cap de Rabast [QC-20]

A classic light station with keepers' houses, service buildings and a 21m (70 ft.) white, octagonal tower stands on Cap de Rabast on the north side of Anticosti Island. It was built on the north side of Anticosti opposite and complementary to Pointe des Monts on the north shore of the St. Lawrence. The station had been automated in the 1970s and, when this photograph was taken in the early 1980s, the windows had been boarded up and the two buildings in front of the tower had assumed the vital functions. Extensive shallow reefs protect the point from storm waves.

Bagot Bluff  QC-21

A square skeleton tower, 15m (50 ft.) high, stands on the northwest side of South Point on Anticosti Island. It marks the site of the old Bagot Bluff light station, first lit in 1871. In the latter days of the original tower, a large double keepers' house with gingerbread trim stood beside a white tower with flying buttresses. By 1980 the house was derelict, the tower decapitated and the station had a desolate air. Today little is left but an automated airport beacon. The map (p.135) shows its position relative to shipping channels between Anticosti and the Gaspé Peninsula.

Southwest Point

QC-16

Close to shipping lanes and abundant limestone and sand for construction, Southwest Point was chosen for Anticosti's first lighthouse (1831). Its massive 24m (80-ft.) tower supported the first rotating light on the St. Lawrence. The lamp burned sperm oil in its first days but soon more economical and efficient fuels were used. From its height of nearly 31m (100 ft.) above the sea, its light was visible for 15 nautical miles.

By the 1970s, the station had been virtually abandoned and the gutted tower, still magnificent in its old age, stood gaunt and empty. For a time, a skeleton tower with airport beacon took over the lighthouse functions. A small graveyard, among the weeds near the shore, reminds the visitor of times when sailors perished offshore and keepers' family members died of untreated maladies. Archival records show that a priest made an annual spring visit to bury the dead washed ashore the previous winter.

By the 1990s, the station had been altogether discontinued. It is accessible on the network of woods roads on Anticosti.

QUEBEC *to* TROIS PISTOLES

Long Pilgrim, Quebec

Grande Isle Kamouraska QC – 23

The south shore of the St. Lawrence from Quebec City to Rimouski is riddled with rocky islands, some standing among sandy shoals and tidal flats. Grande Isle Kamouraska is about 32 kms (20 mi.) upstream from Rivière du Loup. Automation has reduced this station to a skeleton tower and airport beacon. The old tower, built in 1862, and the residence (added in 1913) were sadly decrepit when this photograph was taken in 1980. The hills of the Canadian Shield are in the distance across the St. Lawrence.

White Island Reef QC-24

One of Canada's pure, pillar or caisson lights stands in 6m (20 ft.) of water in the St. Lawrence in the channel opposite Green island (Isle Verte). This is about halfway between Rivière du Loup and Tadoussac at the mouth of the Saguenay River. It replaced Lightship No. 22 east of White Island. The steel shell was designed and built at the Lauzon shipyards in 1954 and was towed out and anchored in 1955. It was a picturesque convoy, with a Coast Guard vessel, four tugs, and a floating caisson moving down the river. Seacocks were opened, the 4,000 ton caisson sank into position, and was fastened to the bottom with stainless steel pins, 3.6m (12 ft) long and 12.5 cms (5") square. The whole cylinder was filled with ballast stone and a reinforced concrete structure, four storeys high, was built on top.

It was a wasp-waisted, steel cylinder with the narrow part at water level to break up winter and spring ice. Its light was some 22m (73 ft.) above the water, and was visible for more than 20 nautical miles. In later years it cut a curious figure with a helicopter landing pad on its very top and the rotating beacon peeking out below. It does not appear in the 1998 List of Lights.

Life on pillar lights was particularly difficult. Even in fine weather there was nowhere to walk or run, no gardens except a window plant or two, no fishing or hunting nearby and no casual visitors. Most pillar lights were not large enough to accommodate families. Particularly frustrating on some were the views of fields and farms, forests and roads, all in the distance, all unreachable. In storms, pillar lights felt completely confining and not a little frightening (see Prince Shoal Pillar).

Red Islet

On a map of Canada, the St. Lawrence River seems to be a wide, clear passageway into the continent. In fact, it requires very careful navigation around its many reefs, shoals and small islands. Two of these hazards, Prince's Shoal and Red Islet—in the channel out from the mouth of the Saguenay River—brought many vessels to grief in earlier times. The tidal currents at this part of the waterway are so irregular that vessels were frequently "deceived as to their situation", as one late-18th-century report phrased it.

A stout stone tower was completed on Red Islet in 1848, constructed with large, beautifully fitted blocks. According to local lore, its fine-grained, grey limestone was brought out from Scotland. This story is quite possibly true in view of this being the day of immigrant ships when a ballasting cargo of stone would be reasonable. (It is known for certain that stone for some of the West Coast lights was brought all the way around Cape Horn in 1860.) Brick was used inside the Red Islet stone tower, and the light platform is supported by a masonry arch. A catoptric (mirror), long-focus system backed the Red Islet light and was still in service into the 1980s, one of the last of its kind in Canada. The old clockwork mechanism is still there, complete with the shaft for the weights. The original 14-sided lantern house has 72 panes of polished "lighthouse glass" in three tiers in a red metal frame under its polygonal roof with a ventilation cap and an arrow and feathers weathervane.

This beautifully finished stone tower with its 18m (60 ft.) height partly disguised by its stout shape and horizontal ribs; and its broad, flat, many-sided lamphouse with the old reflector still turning after all these years makes this light very special.

Prince Shoal

Prince Shoal is another hazard to St. Lawrence navigation. It is a shallow sandy area directly opposite the mouth of the Saguenay River off Tadoussac, between Quebec City and Rivière du Loup. To deal with the challenge of shoals, lighthouse builders had three approaches: they could anchor a lightship—really a floating lighthouse—on or near the hazard; they could sink steel pilings that would support a lighthouse on a platform above the water; or they could sink a caisson into the soft bottom.

In 1964, a caisson was placed on Prince Shoal, designed to withstand 8-m (25-ft.) waves. It was also carefully shaped with a slender "wasp waist" to break up drifting river ice in winter and spring. It was soon to face a mighty test. On Christmas Day, 1966, a wild storm, perhaps the worst of the century, lashed the St. Lawrence. The three keepers on Prince Shoal watched in horror as waves mounted higher than the platform. Their isolated perch began to shake, windows started caving in and destruction spread through the upper level under the onslaught of waves 12m (40 ft.) high. The men sent out a distress signal but were not recued until half a day later when the weather cleared enough to allow a helicopter to land. By storm's end, Prince Shoal lighthouse was in a shambles and even the lamphouse was broken.

Repaired and fortified, Prince Shoal lighthouse sits atop its round caisson with all station functions in a round house above the first platform. Its roof is extended outward to make a slightly larger helicopter landing pad. Its round steel light tower is placed off to one side and is surmounted by a lamphouse with inward sloping glass panes and a flat roof. The fog alarm is unusual with three alarms pointing in different directions and blowing in sequence. Prince Shoal was the site of an experiment using high power Xenon bulbs—each with 32,000,000 candle power—but they proved to be too bright. They were relegated for use in very dull weather, with ordinary incandescent bulbs used most of the time.

Isle Verte

Erected in 1809, the lighthouse at Isle Verte (Green Island) is the third oldest surviving light in Canada. It sits in its original form on a low, rocky point on the seaward side of Isle Verte, 29 kms (18 mi.) northeast of Rivière du Loup. Designed to warn ships of the treacherous shoals and currents off the mouth of the Saguenay River, it was the only light serving the St. Lawrence for twenty years. Isle Verte is predated only by Sambro, near Halifax (1759) and Gibraltar Point on Toronto Island (1808) (which is preserved only as a monument).

Although construction began in 1806, the original circular stone tower on Green Island—as it was then known—was not completed until 1809. It had a twelve-sided lanternhouse, and keepers had to tend a battery of 13 lamps and reflectors. The station's first keeper, Charles Hambleton, died in 1827 and was replaced by a young apprentice pilot and seaman of Scottish descent, Robert Lindsay from Quebec City. Lindsay's appointment began an unmatched family record of service that lasted until 1964. Generation after generation of Lindsays minded the Isle Verte light, the technology growing and changing with them. For 137 years, they guided brigs and schooners, bulk carriers and luxury liners through all weather and seasons. The venerable old light was declared a National Historic Site in 1974. It is can be reached by an intermittent ferry opposite from the village of L'Isle Verte.

St. Lawrence, South Shore, Trois Pistoles *to* Gaspé

Father Point (Point au Père), Quebec

Isle Bicquette

Pilots were needed to lead the ships through a group of tricky offshore islands twenty kms (12 nautical mi.) upriver from Father Point (Pointe au Père). The outermost of these islands is home to the Isle Bicquette light station with a beacon that shines for many miles in each direction. It is a massive, round masonry tower some 22.6m (74 ft.) high clad in wood. Its thick walls are evident in its deep-set windows at each level. Atop the tower is a classic Bernier, Bénard and Turenne round lamphouse with curved glass windows, a large ventilation cap and weathervane. When I visited in 1980, cannon from the days when they fired fog warnings were still on the grounds, and remainders of the old gas mantle lamps were still inside the lighthouse. The original 1st Order Fresnel lens rotated in its cage as it had for nearly a century and a half. A tall, radio mast and electronic fog horns foretold the coming automation which was completed in 1981. Some of the buildings have since been dismantled.

This beautiful old light was built in 1843-44, one of three lights built below Quebec City in response to petitions from ship owners and mariners. The other two at Red Islet and Stone Pillar have also survived.

Father Point

As ships proceeded upriver, they picked up river pilots at Father Point (Point au Père), on the south shore near Rimouski, to guide them through the treacherous passages. The first lighthouse was built here in 1859. Destroyed by fire in 1867, it was immediately replaced by a wooden tower. In 1909, one of Colonel Anderson's flying buttressed reinforced concrete towers came into service. Its 2nd Order Fresnel lens sent its beams for 15 nautical miles out over the St. Lawrence. In 1980, its functions were assumed by a steel lattice tower and airport beacon. The old tower soon began to deteriorate. Weathering paint revealed the method of construction: successive levels of cement poured one on top of the other (see Caribou Island light, p.197).

No longer in use, the old tower's lens is covered against the sun. The station is being restored and operated by the "Cooperative Association Le Musée de la Mer de Pointe-au-Père". The grounds have been redone with old anchors, cannon and other relics, picnic tables and a children's playground. The keeper's house is a museum. It was designated a National Historic Site in 1974. This station is readily accessible by a short side road from the main coastal road (Route 132) just east of Rimouski.

Pointe Mitis QC-29

About 18 kms (12 mi.) northeast of Mont Joli, a reinforced concrete lighthouse stands on a bar called Pointe Mitis. The first light was built here in 1874. The present hexagonal tower stands some 17m (52 ft.) high. It serves as guide to coastwise and river shipping and is the major coastwise lighthouse halfway between Father Point and Matane, a distance of 75 kms (45 mi.).

Cap Chat

A lighthouse station was installed at Cap Chat in 1871 as part of a string of lights along the south side of of the St. Lawrence estuary. The present tower was built in 1909 and its 3rd Order lens still functions. The Bernier, Bénard and Turenne lamphouse rests on a short, square wooden tower. Although the tower is only 10m (33 ft.) high, its clifftop position means that it is 40m (133 ft.) above the sea. The station is automated and includes a bank of electronic foghorns. Like all the lights along the coastal road, the station is on mainline hydro.

Cap Chat's name comes from the cat-like profile of a nearby rocky point. This is behind the old stone magazine which was built to house the explosives for the fog guns of earlier times.

This station is now under the management of the Germain-Lemieux Museum and is largely

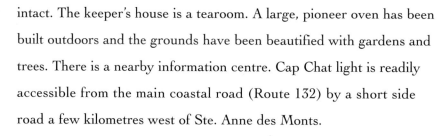

intact. The keeper's house is a tearoom. A large, pioneer oven has been built outdoors and the grounds have been beautified with gardens and trees. There is a nearby information centre. Cap Chat light is readily accessible from the main coastal road (Route 132) by a short side road a few kilometres west of Ste. Anne des Monts.

Rivière à la Martre

Rivière à la Martre lighthouse is an imposing, all red light tower perched on the edge of the coastal cliffs. It is situated about halfway between Rimouski and the Gaspé on the south side of the St. Lawrence estuary. Its rotating Fresnel lens has four dioptric lenses that produce four flashes and a pause each minute. On the seaward side, a broad white stripe from base to tower makes a distinctive daymark. Served by local power lines, the light station is entirely automated. All the buildings have been painted red and now house various museum functions. The lighthouse is right beside the main coastal road (Route 132) and offers a splendid view of the St. Lawrence to the north.

ST. LAWRENCE, NORTH SHORE, TADOUSSAC *to* STRAIT *of* BELLE ISLE

Great Cawee Island, Quebec

Pointe des Monts

For more than 81 years, the Fafard family—fathers and sons in succession—tended the lighthouse at Pointe des Monts on the north shore of the St. Lawrence River estuary, 19 kms (12 mi.) east of Godbout. Until the Quebec 138 shore road was built, the light station's only access was by sea. Today the light revolves from atop a steel, skeleton tower. The old light tower, keeper's house and grounds are now a museum and park.

Still largely in its original form, the lighthouse is a massive, round, 27m (90 ft.) tower. It is 12m (40 ft.) in diameter at the base and tapers to 6m (20 ft.) at the bottom of the platform, with walls 1.8m (6 ft.) thick at the bottom and 0.6m (2 ft.) at the lantern level. When construction began in 1829, contractors tried to use the local granitic rock but they found it difficult to work. As an alternative, they brought limestone down river from near Montreal. The polygonal copper lantern accommodated an array of 13 Argand lamps, each with its own polished reflector. At the end of the 19th-century, a new lamp and Fresnel lens system were installed. The unusually large, scrolled supports for the roof are still visible. When the tower was clad in wood and shingled, the tall, 14-paned windows were framed on the outside, giving a pleasing effect.

The old white tower is nicely set off by its daymark of two broad, horizontal red stripes and by the nearby keeper's residence with its bright red roof. Today it is easy to forget that the lighthouse was built in response to the procession of horrifying shipwrecks along this unmarked coast more than a century and a half ago.

Carrousel Island QC-32

The early days of World War II brought a rude awakening to the sleepy little fishing and lumbering village of Seven Islands (Sept Isles) on the north shore of the St. Lawrence estuary. First, in order to patrol the Gulf of St. Lawrence and to train pilots, an airport was built. After the war, interest developed in the iron ranges deep in the hinterland to the north. What started as a trickle soon became a flood of prospectors, geologists (my younger self included), construction workers and, in the early 1950s, railway workers. Suddenly, in 1954, after several years of feverish construction, Seven Islands became a major shipping port. Every day the new railway brought thousands of tons of iron ore for shipment to Great Lakes ports and overseas. Completion of the St. Lawrence Seaway was hurried to accommodate this new industry.

This is why an island-studded bay on a remote coast became a port for a steady procession of large ships. Carrousel Island is on the outside edge of the archipelago that gives the name to the bay and the city. It has had a lighthouse since 1870 to aid local traffic along the north shore.

When this picture was taken in the early 1980s, the station was still staffed, but the octagonal concrete tower with its angular, 1960s aluminum lamphouse had been put aside. The functions of the station had been assumed by the skeleton tower, airport beacon, small control buildings and the bank of electronic horns. The station was destaffed long ago and parts of it have been demolished.

Perroquet Island

Nearly flat-lying limestones lie on the ancient rocks of the Precambrian Shield all along the St. Lawrence River valley. The Mingan Islands—a few miles west of Havre St. Pierre opposite the west end of Anticosti Island—are erosional remnants of limestone beds that lie just above sea level. On Perroquet Island, a white, octagonal tower with red lanternhouse advises ships of the treacherous shoals and islands in the vicinity.

Now automated (as are all lights along this coast) there are only remnants of the station left to remind visitors of the families who lived on this small, isolated island beginning in 1888. It was tough living for the keepers and their families until the closing of the station each winter when navigation ended on the frozen St. Lawrence.

Perroquet Island is now part of Mingan Islands National Park. The surrounding shorelines and low islands are renowned for their erosional remnants of flat limestone in a variety of shapes on tidal flats and along shore cliffs. The area is a haven for shore birds and the limestone provides a home for a whole suite of unusual botanical species.

Natashquan Point

The north shore of the Gulf of St. Lawrence is cut by major rivers running down to it from the Canadian Shield to the north. When these rivers encounter glacial deposits common in the area, they winnow out the sands and fine gravels and deposit them at their mouths along the sea. Natashquan Point lighthouse is thus surrounded by long sandy beaches, often black with magnetite, with incredible patterns of curving sand ridges marking former river channels and beaches.

The lighthouse was built in 1914 on a terrace just back from the shoreline. It is a sturdy, white, hexagonal tower with joined buttresses, typical of its time. When the lights were automated all along the coast, Natashquan became the monitoring station for their automatic signals. Banks of glowing lights informed the keeper of the condition of the surrounding stations' operations and when to send for maintenance help. Natashquan is about 80 kms (50 mi.) east of Sept Isles as the crow flies and is not easily accessible.

Flat Island

No ship at sea ever saw this outpost of navigation from such a view. This is an aerial view of the low, rocky Flat Islands on the north side of the St. Lawrence east of Sept Isles. Appropriately named, these barren, rocky islands have been marked with a lighthouse since 1913. Today, the automated station is home to little more than a skeleton tower and airport beacon 24.4m (80 ft.) above the sea.

Long Point, Ontario

ONTARIO

O ntario has a surprising variety of lighthouses for a province landlocked except for a salt water northern coastline at the south end of Hudson's Bay. The secret lies in the St. Lawrence waterway and the Great Lakes. In the earliest days of Ontario's settlement, the St. Lawrence River was the avenue into the interior, and shipping routes developed throughout the Great Lakes. Some of the earliest lighthouses in Canada were built in Ontario in the very early 19th century. The light at Gibraltar Point on Toronto Island (1809) is the second oldest surviving lighthouse in Canada.

Great Lakes shipping advanced with the completion of two canals in the early 20th century: the first Welland Canal, between Lakes Ontario and Erie, and then the Sault Canal, between Superior and Huron. The completion of the second Welland Canal in 1931 meant that large "lakers" could transit all the lakes. The completion of the St. Lawrence Seaway in 1954 opened the interior of the continent to ocean shipping and "salties" from all over the world.

Lighthouses in Ontario run the whole gamut of sizes, shapes, function and architecture. Arguably the most beautiful lighthouse in Canada is on a low, small satellite of Caribou Island, well out in Lake Superior, with its slender 30m (100 ft.) tower supported by graceful, flying buttresses. The design is shared by the Estevan light on the rainy, west coast of Vancouver Island. Another, though smaller, is at Michipicoten Island (East) on the northeastern corner of Lake Superior. In other locations, simple, square, wooden dwellings were built with a light tower on top. Several of these have survived. Curious-looking lights sit on wave-washed Red Rock in Georgian Bay, and at Gros Cap, just northwest of Sault Ste. Marie, built on a concrete crib to withstand Lake Superior's winter ice. Another unusual light is found at Windmill Point on the St. Lawrence near Prescott. It has performed as a lighthouse since its functions as a mill were abandoned in 1873. Some of the islands on the north shore of Lake Superior are home to what can only be described as remote lights, perhaps surprising for a province as well populated as Ontario. In addition to major lights, hundreds of small lights, channel markers, buoys and range lights dot difficult shores, such as the east side of Georgian Bay and the river channels between the lakes.

Today, the lighthouses of Ontario have been automated and destaffed, as have lighthouses all over the world. Even the sounds of the faithful, diesel generators are gone, replaced by silent, solar panels and banks of long-life batteries. One peculiarity of automation is the continued operation of many lights during the winter, even though shipping stops when the Great Lakes freeze. As car owners know, batteries will go dead if they are left in storage for long periods, so they need to be run during the winter months. And solar cells require no maintenance in order to work in the winter sunlight. The batteries and the solar panels are therefore left to shine out over the frozen lakes, even when no one is around to tend them, or to see them.

ONTARIO

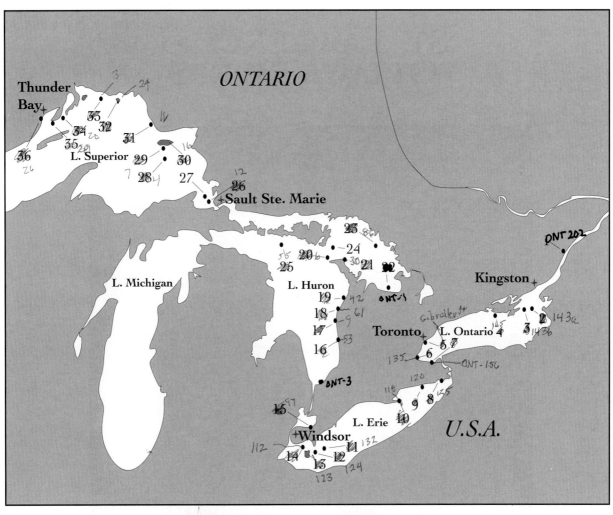

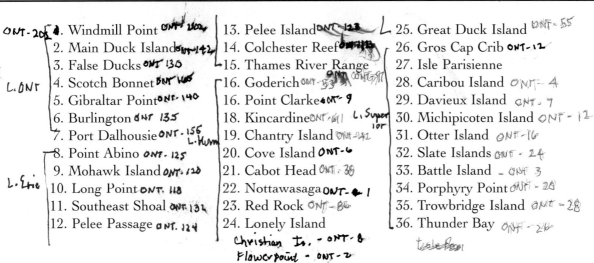

ONT-202 1. Windmill Point ONT-202
2. Main Duck Island ONT-142
3. False Ducks ONT 130
L.ONT 4. Scotch Bonnet ONT-105
5. Gibraltar Point ONT-140
6. Burlington ONT 135
7. Port Dalhousie ONT-156
L.Huron
L.Erie 8. Point Abino ONT-125
9. Mohawk Island ONT-120
10. Long Point ONT-118
11. Southeast Shoal ONT-132
12. Pelee Passage ONT-124

13. Pelee Island ONT-123
14. Colchester Reef ONT-123
15. Thames River Range
16. Goderich ONT-53 ONT CONT-97
16. Point Clarke ONT-9
18. Kincardine ONT-61 L.Super 105
19. Chantry Island ONT-142
20. Cove Island ONT-6
21. Cabot Head ONT-38
22. Nottawasaga ONT-1
23. Red Rock ONT-86
24. Lonely Island
Christian Is. - ONT-8
Flowerpoint - ONT-2

25. Great Duck Island ONT-55
26. Gros Cap Crib ONT-12
27. Isle Parisienne
28. Caribou Island ONT-4
29. Davieux Island ONT-7
30. Michipicoten Island ONT-12
31. Otter Island ONT-16
32. Slate Islands ONT-24
33. Battle Island - ONT 3
34. Porphyry Point ONT-20
35. Trowbridge Island ONT-28
36. Thunder Bay ONT-26

teoleResol

ST. LAWRENCE &
OTTAWA RIVERS

Ottawa River, Ontario

Windmill Point

One of the most unusual lighthouses in Canada is on the St. Lawrence River, a mile east of Prescott, Ontario. Here, a massive, 19m (62 ft.) limestone tower, topped with a meagre lamphouse is unique in both lighthouse architecture and history. Originally built as a windmill, it was bought by the Department of Marine in 1873 and converted to a lighthouse. An ornate platform and routine lanternhouse were added on top. It was equipped with multiple kerosene burners with reflectors and showed a fixed white light. Later, a 5th Order dioptric system was installed.

Commemorative plaques posted here do not relate specifically to the windmill or to the lighthouse. In 1838, a group of rebels held out in this great stone tower in what was called the "Battle of the Windmill. Guns brought in from Kingston ended the seige and left 35 dead and many more wounded. Of the 157 rebels captured, 12 were later executed, 60 exiled to Australia and the rest expelled from the country. A plaque honouring the Polish soldiers who fought here was affixed by the Polish-Canadian community. This unusual site is alongside the shore road just east of Prescott.

LAKE ONTARIO

Keeper at Main Duck Island, Ontario

Main Duck Island

Main Duck Island, about 32 kms (20 mi.) due south of Kingston, is one of a string of low islands lying across the entrance of the St. Lawrence River at the east end of Lake Ontario. Just inside the Canadian border, Main Duck was owned for many years by John Foster Dulles, Secretary of State for the United States, who spent his last days there. He deeded the island as a bird sanctuary and so it remains.

A light was installed on the island in the early 1800s. Built in 1914, the existing reinforced-concrete lighthouse is an octagonal tower with seven levels up to the lantern platform from a multi-layered plinth. Now the Fresnel is gone, solar power runs the equipment and no one lives or works there any more.

When I first visited Main Duck in 1977, the keeper took the helicopter pilot and me down to see his "hobby" in one of the side buildings. Not many keepers build their own airplanes. But there it was—an airplane—framed in and awaiting Department of Transport inspection.

There are the hardships on light stations and there are the adventures. Every so often an extraordinary event may break the regular flow of life. One such event took place on Main Duck Island light station during a Royal visit to Canada a few years ago. On a day carefully arranged in secrecy, the Royal Yacht *Britannia* came into view a little way down the island and anchored. A friendly R.C.M.P. officer soon appeared at the door of the keeper's residence. A little later, Queen Elizabeth in kerchief and jacket, with Prince Philip beside her, led a relaxed and happy walking party along the path to their door.

With a broad smile, the Queen joined the keeper and his wife in a hastily brewed cup of tea and a relaxed and folksy chat. *Britannia* sailed away later that day, after a happy day of picnicing and respite on the "deserted" Main Duck.

False Ducks

A string of islands crosses the east end of Lake Ontario from Prince Edward to Stony Point in New York State. A lighthouse was placed on Swetman Island, near the Canadian end, as early as 1828. The station is called False Ducks, presumably in reference to the much larger Main Duck light, 15 kms (9 mi.) across the channel to the east. In 1965, the old tower was literally pulled down by using a ship and a long cable, leaving behind debris and an old foundation. Its replacement is a slim, hexagonal tower with a top that looks like an airport control tower. The white tower has a conspicuous daymark of three red bands. Nearby is another structure that looks like a lighthouse but is a memorial to merchant sailors. Access is by boat.

Scotch Bonnet

In 1853-55, a robust light tower with attached residence was built of blocky limestone on Scotch Bonnet, a small, flat island off the western shore of the Picton Peninsula in eastern Lake Ontario. The island is so low that a retaining wall was built on the flat limestone beds to protect the station and to provide a small, grassy area. Scotch Bonnet tower was discontinued in 1959 and left to the circling gulls and the weather. This photograph, taken in 1977, demonstrates that masonry is only as strong as its mortar. It also shows how effectively wind-driven rain penetrates and destroys the most exposed

side. The lesson for lighthouse watchers is how justified the lighthouse engineers were to clad masonry towers—both brick and stone—in protective wood and shingles, as they did at dozens of towers, including at Prim Point, P.E.I., Point Amour, Newfoundland and Presqu'ile, Ontario. The remains of the lamphouse show its diamond window pattern, fairly uncommon in Canadian lights. Access is by boat.

Gibraltar Point

In 1808, artificers of the 41st Regiment built a masonry tower on Toronto Island's Gibraltar Point. The hexagonal tower has limestone walls with a slight collar to mark the beginning of tapering of the walls to a collar marking the platform level of the earliest lighthouse. In 1832, 4.5m (15 ft.) of slightly different masonry extended the tower to its current height. Here, a ten-sided lanternhouse, installed around 1875, housed the rotating lights 22.5m (75 ft.) above lake level.

Although long out of service, this is the second oldest original tower in Canada (only Sambro is older). It is preserved in a park setting by the City of Toronto. It is easily accessible by taking the Hanlan's ferry from the foot of Yonge Street in downtown Toronto. Once across, it is a short walk to this historic lighthouse in its peaceful setting, yet so close to the swirling city traffic.

Burlington

When, in 1838, a limestone masonry tower was built on the sand and gravel bar between Burlington Bay and the west end of Lake Ontario, it stood alone. Since then, a principal highway and swing bridge, power lines and the Burlington Skyway have overwhelmed the 17m (55 ft.) tower, making it look like a tiny accoutrement to all those steel and concrete structures. It was closed in 1961 and only strong protests from local historical interests saved the old tower from demolition.

Typical of its day, the lighthouse tower has massive walls, probably 1.8m (6 ft.) thick at the base, tapered slightly to its platform with tall, deep-set, narrow windows marking each of its four, interior landings. The lantern is polygonal with tall glass panes. The ventilation cap with wind vane on top remains from oil lamp days.

Port Dalhousie

The entry to Port Dalhousie—on the west end of Lake Ontario near the foot of the Welland Canal—has two, handsome, wooden lighthouses that function as range lights. The inner light is a 16.8m (56 ft.) octagonal tower with gently sloping, shingled sides; a red, 12-sided lanternhouse enclosing a "beehive" lens; and a beaver weather vane on top. Such beavers are rare in Canadian lights but others can be found on Belle Isle (North) and Ile Parisienne. The outer range is a square, tapering tower 9.6m (32 ft.) high. This pair of handsome lights is accessible from streets in Port Dalhousie.

Lake Erie *&*
Lake St. Clair

Mohawk Island, Ontario

Point Abino

Perhaps the most bizarre lighthouse design in Canada is this structure near the eastern end of Lake Erie built in 1918. A wonderful exercise in sculpted concrete, it is beautiful in its way and is certainly unique. When this picture was taken in 1981, the Fresnel lens still rotated in its ten-sided lantern-house. The square tower with multiple windows rises from a collar-type plinth just above roof level of the service building, and flares out gracefully to support the platform. The service building sits on a raised concrete island, like a royal barge in shallow water, with stairs leading from a fancy front door to a passageway across the shallows to the shore. The site is easily accessible from the main road and side roads between Port Colborne and Fort Erie.

Mohawk Island

A sad little monument to times gone by sits on a low island, just southeast of Port Maitland on the north side of Lake Erie. A beautifully constructed masonry tower and attached residence have decayed here since being abandoned in 1969. The round tower has narrow slit windows marking five levels to the decapitated platform. Its masonry is of exceptional quality and even after decades of neglect, the ruins still show beautiful technique in the stone-framed windows and arched doorway. Although the station has been discontinued, there is a small flashing light in place of the former lanternhouse.

Long Point

In 1915-16, a slender white 100-foot tower was built with its feet in the lagoon between two sand ridges of Long Point. It is the warning beacon for extensive sandy shoals and for Long Point itself, sticking out for several miles from the north shore of Lake Erie between Port Burwell and Port Dover.

The first light on Long Point was a stone tower 15m (50 ft.) high built on a crib of massive timbers. Illustrating the perils of building on sandbars, this tower only lasted a decade before erosion took its toll. A second light was erected in 1843 and lasted until being replaced by the existing one.

As with all original Canadian lighthouses, the first lights here started life with multiple fixed lamps and reflectors that were later converted to rotating units with approximately six lamps and mirrors. When the new tower was built, it was equipped with a rotating Fresnel lens system. It now works with an airport beacon-style light running on main-line hydro.

Southeast Shoal

On this calm, hazy, summer's day, it was difficult to imagine the station in a Lake Erie storm with passing ships fighting to keep to the channels while waters raged all round.

The southernmost point in Canada is on Pelee Island in western Lake Erie, which is surprisingly at the same latitude as northern California. Lake Erie is the shallowest of the Great Lakes. Pelee Island is but one of many islands and shoals—hazards to shipping—near the mouth of the Detroit River. Several ship channels exist but the main one passes between Point Pelee on the mainland and Pelee Island. The lighthouse history in the passage began with a tower built on the northeast point of the Island in 1833 (see Pelee Island, p.178). These days its functions are performed by two caisson-type lights called Pelee Passage and Southeast Shoal.

Southeast Shoal light station is on a massive square-built caisson. It is surrounded by large boulders at water level and has inward sloping sides on its lower portion to counter drifting ice. The station is a three-storey building with helicopter pad on top and has two parallel, vertical, black stripes on each white flank as its daymark. In its last days as a staffed station, two keepers alternated with two others in two-week shifts.

Pelee Passage

One of the main channels for ships transitting the west end of Lake Erie is the Pelee Passage between Point Pelee on the mainland to the north and Pelee Island. In 1902, a light was built on a caisson-type pier on the north end of Middle Ground Shoal, well off Point Pelee, replacing an earlier light built closer to the point. It was rebuilt in the 1970s to accommodate a helicopter landing pad, its light tower set off to one corner. The plain, white, cylindrical tower holds a small platform with railing and an unusual lanternhouse with glass panes sloping inward towards the base, as airport control towers do. It has long been automated and destaffed.

Pelee Island

This tower, the second in Lake Erie, was built in 1833 in the first attempt to light the Pelee Passage between Pelee Island and Point Pelee on the mainland. It suffered from poor positioning and a lack of maintenance and was badly damaged in the uprising in 1837. Refurbished and relit, it was never very satisfactory. In the end, it was discontinued after a larger and better light was placed off the end of Pelee Point in 1861. The stump of the old stone tower remains half hidden in the trees on the north point.

Colchester Reef

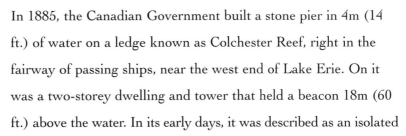

In 1885, the Canadian Government built a stone pier in 4m (14 ft.) of water on a ledge known as Colchester Reef, right in the fairway of passing ships, near the west end of Lake Erie. On it was a two-storey dwelling and tower that held a beacon 18m (60 ft.) above the water. In its early days, it was described as an isolated station, presumably because of its caisson-like situation several miles from shore. It was a fixed white light with a 3rd Order dioptric lens system, visible in all directions for about 22 kms (14 mi.). In 1977, a skeleton tower with an automatic light replaced the tower on the old repaired masonry base.

Thames River Range

A light of some type was established early—probably prior to 1800—at the mouth of the Thames River in southwestern Ontario. This stone structure was constructed in 1818, and served until automation in 1966. It remained derelict for most of a decade but was then rescued and restored by the local Thames River Conservation Authority. The site has a remarkable history in that members of the same family, the Cartiers, were keepers there for 150 years.

LAKE HURON & GEORGIAN BAY

Nottawasaga, Ontario

Goderich

The first lighthouse on Lake Huron was built at Goderich in 1847. It was placed near the cliff front 30m (100 ft.) above the water, along the north-south trending shore. A squat, square, stone tower only 6m (20 ft.) high supports a 12-sided lanternhouse. The light is 43m (143 ft.) above lake level. Through numerous technological changes, the lighthouse has served shore navigation and marked the entry to Goderich for 150 years. Easy to visit, it is not far off main coastal route 21.

Point Clark

Point Clark lighthouse was one of six, tall, stone towers completed in 1859 on Lake Huron, two on the west side of the Bruce Peninsula, one on the northern tip and three on the shore of Georgian Bay. They were of the same general pattern as towers completed at Point Amour on the Strait of Belle Isle, West Point of Anticosti, and Cap des Rosiers, on the tip of the Gaspé Peninsula. They were referred to as "Imperial towers" although it is not known just why that is. It may be because they followed British plans. Point Clark is north of Goderich and not far south of Kincardine. Even though its base is close to water level, the 26m (87 ft.) light warns of shoals a few kilometres offshore and can be seen far beyond in all directions.

The walls are two metres thick (7 ft.) at its base and taper gently upwards. Massive, rough-dressed, 19-inch blocks of limestone, probably of local origin, are laid in regular courses to the base of the platform. The top of the tower supports a masonry base for the 12-sided lanternhouse with its rivetted copper, sectioned dome. Its original light used a 2nd Order Fresnel lens system and oil lamps, long since replaced by modern lights and lenses. Point Clark, along with Chantry and others along that shore will eventually come under the administration of the Bruce County Museum with local groups in each place doing the restoration and maintenance. (For the most complete description of the Imperial lights, see Cove Island on the northern tip of the Bruce Peninsula.)

Kincardine

Unlike the incredibly complex eastern shore of Georgian Bay, the eastern shore of Lake Huron is smooth and uncluttered. A few scattered indentations make small harbours and one of these is at Kincardine. It is marked by range lights, the back range being an outstanding example of a light tower sprouting from a corner of the residence. Kincardine is the largest of its kind left in Canada. It is also the most garishly painted: red all around the windows and some of the trim boards, as well as the lanternhouse, the platform and its bracket supports.

The back light tower itself is a tapering octagonal wooden structure rising from the seaward corner of a large two-story building. It is hard to know just where the tower begins on this complex piece of architecture, as it combines tower, service building and foundation storey. Brackets support the platform with its large, multi-sided lanternhouse, tall rectangular windows and flashing light.

The whole makes for a commanding structure in the inside harbour. It was built in 1881 and is listed as 19.2m (64 ft.) high, its light 24m (80 ft.) above water. It is readily accessible from waterside Kincardine.

Chantry Island

The old tower on Chantry Island was completed by Public Works in 1859. It is visible from the mainland just south of Southampton on the west shore of the Bruce Peninsula. It was one of the six "Imperial towers" built from 1857-60 in Lake Huron and Georgian Bay. At 26m (86 ft.), it is an imposing structure with its rough-dressed, heavy, limestone blocks. The tower is whitewashed and without daymarks. Its original lens system was removed in 1954 when the last keeper, Cameron Spencer, retired and an automatic, flashing light was installed. In 1954, the island was declared a bird sanctuary.

Its easy accessibility by small boats left it highly vulnerable to vandalism and the residence and grounds quickly deteriorated. However, a local group from the Southhampton Museum has taken on the restoration of the site. Plans include refurbishing the residence, building walkways and trails and restricting and supervising visits during the bird season. (More details about "Imperial towers" are included under the Cove Island Station.)

Cove Island

Near the end of my third visit to Cove Island light station in the summer of 1998, I lay in a shady spot on the front steps of a boarded up residence awaiting transportation. Nearby was Cove's gracefully tapering, round, stone tower with its red polygonal lamphouse, one of the most beautiful of all Canadian lighthouses. It was particularly dazzling on this sunny day with its pristine coat of new white paint. The breeze was gentle and the blissful silence was broken only by the chatter of terns on the rocks just offshore and the rumbling of a passing ferry. In that peaceful setting I could feel the history that this lighthouse has seen.

Almost 150 years ago, the burgeoning shipping trade with lumber from Georgian Bay required a major lighthouse at the entrance to the Bay from Lake Huron. In late 1855, work began on this site. In 1856, a crew of masons, stone cutters, and labourers quarried local limestone, dressed it and finished the tower. It was not capped with its proper light and dome until 1860. Cove Island was one of six "Imperial" towers completed at that time in Lake Huron. Cove still has its polygonal lamphouse with decorative lion's heads holding up the gutter system. Inside, six vertical Fresnel lenses with six spaces between, sit on a rotating frame producing a steady light that flashes as the lenses come into focus every six seconds. As we approached in our helicopter, we could see it from 8 kms (5 mi.) away, even on a sunny day.

Cove Island interior

Inside the massive stone walls, the first flight of steps follows the curving masonry. On successive levels, straight stairs lead from platform to platform. The massive timber joists that hold up the floors are set right into the masonry walls and are clearly visible on each level. Nearing the top, one can hear the hum of the electric motor and its gear box—that turn the light—the only sound beyond the wind. Remnants of the old weight-driven clockwork are still visible as is the enclosed weight shaft now carrying electric cables and wires through the floors. A lone electric bulb sits at the centre of the rotating lens system where, in other times, a succession of different oil and vapour lamps fueled the beacon light.

In the fog alarm building, two Lister diesel engines with their compressors, so marvelously dependable in lighthouses all over the world, sit quietly near the huge air tanks with pipes leading to the old diaphone horn sticking through the wall. A little way along the beach of limestone slabs, sits a

Cove Island lenses

battery of electronic horns that sound a higher-pitched, but little loved warning. The old, low-pitched, diaphone "groaners" were much easier to listen to and carried farther. Lighthouse legend tells of Keeper William Spears, who found it hard to bear the high-pitched squeal of the new electronic horn installed that year (1971). In desperation one foggy night, he switched it off and cranked up his old friend, the diaphone, and listened contentedly to its booming bass voice.

Automation slowly caught up to Cove Island light station. By the late 1970s almost all functions were automated and the keepers were there more as caretakers and watchmen. Power for the station was supplied through a submarine cable and land lines so this seemingly remote station didn't even have to generate its own power any more. The last of the keepers in Georgian Bay, Jack Vaughan, was removed from Cove Island in 1991. He had looked after the station with exceptional pride and it remains in excellent shape. Here and there among the limestone walls a few of the flowers lovingly planted by keepers remind visitors of other times. This station should one day make a fine park.

Cabot Head

By 1860, the Cove Island lighthouse marked the south side of the main channel into Georgian Bay. As vessels entered the Bay, then turned south down its western shore, it was easy to come to grief along the unmarked, ragged limestone shore. After numerous disasters in the 1860s and 70s, lighthouse authorities erected a lighthouse station at the end of the landmark limestone bluffs of Cabot Head, where a small harbour, Wingfield Inlet, offered the only safe anchorage for miles.

The station—complete with steam fog horn—opened for the season in 1896. A new air-driven diaphone was installed after a fire destroyed the original in 1907. The diaphone lasted until 1972 when electronic horns were installed. The old tower was removed in 1972 and its functions taken over by a steel tower and revolving light. Just inside the inlet where she was run ashore, the remains of the *Gargantua* lie slowly decaying in the summer sun.

Cabot Head keepers stayed for unusually long periods. Howard Boyle and his wife lived there from 1926 to 1951 and left a legacy of hand-built stone walls and gardens, and ornamental trees. Harry Hopkins and his family stayed from 1951 to 1982. The last keeper left in 1988. Now a local society operates an interpretative centre at the Cabot Head station. "Friends of Cabot Head," has reconstructed the old light tower, refurbished the residence, tidied the grounds and continue to work to ensure its preservation. The site is accessible by side roads leading off Route 11 on the Bruce Peninsula, through Dyer Bay and along the shore. The Cabot Head reconstruction is a wonderful example of what local groups can do to preserve and celebrate their lighthouse history.

Nottawasaga Island

The "Imperial" towers of Lake Huron are outstanding among Canadian lighthouses with their tall, limestone towers, still standing after a century and a half of service. Nottawasaga is one of these towers, three kms (1.9 mi.) from the harbour at Collingwood. The gleaming white tower, resident water birds and the green wooded island and white limestone shores make a beautiful sight on a sunny day. As with so many lights on Canadian shores, it was born of shipwreck, death and loss of cargo.

By 1850, traffic on Lake Huron and in and out of Georgian Bay was rapidly growing, with settlement coming into the area from the south, roads and railroads poking northward to Collingwood, and outgoing lumber cargoes. The near absence of lights in Lake Huron, and the abundant islands and reefs of Georgian Bay made navigation hazardous. The ever-increasing toll of wrecks made several lights imperative. The usefulness of Nottawasaga, first lit in 1858, was immediately apparent. The

log of George Collins, its keeper from 1860 to 1890, tells of rescue after rescue, of wrecks avoided and more than 50 lives saved.

Today the residence is in ruins, and the gardens and grounds are completely over-grown. Only a few brave plants from earlier days struggle among the bushes and weeds. The French-made fixed lens gave way to a revolving light run by weights wound regularly by the keeper. The tower remained until 1959 when a fire destroyed the residence. At that point, the light was converted to acetylene, the weights and clockwork were removed and the first steps were taken toward automation. The process was complete in 1984. Now a white light flashes out every ten seconds, its power coming from a solar panel and a bank of batteries. In fine weather Nottawasaga Island is accessible by boat.

Red Rock

Glaciers moving over the land in the Georgian Bay region in the last million years scraped away all loose materials, and scratched and polished the bedrock. About 10,000 years ago, the area around Parry Sound was flooded by post-glacial ancestors of Lake Huron. Today, the ancient rocks of the Canadian Shield form a shoreline dotted with smooth, rounded islands, deep inlets and thousands of rock-lined shoals and shallows. While heaven for the wandering boater, it is full of barely hidden perils, and its bottom is strewn with wrecks, anchors and propellers.

In the middle of the 19th century, Parry Sound welcomed scores of vessels carrying the products of sawmills that were springing up all along the shore. The need for aids to navigation became acute and, by 1870, a light was placed on nearby Old Tower Rock. It lasted only a few years before it was wrecked in a storm. A second attempt was made on Red Rock in 1881.

Its location was useful, but it was no more than a bare, rounded boss of smooth granite, a few feet above calm water level, so a foundation was built and a lighthouse installed on that. Photographs show that the 1881 lighthouse looked exactly like the Indian Head (P.E.I.) Light (see photo p.110) built in 1871. In heavy storms, the whole station was covered in a welter of breaking seas. A masonry and concrete-filled steel cylinder, 13m (41 ft.) in diameter and 4m (13 ft.) high, was glued to the rock with inset steel rods. The odd-shaped reinforced-concrete structure we see today was later placed on that.

In the 1970s, a helicopter landing pad was placed like an umbrella on top, its beacon peeking out from underneath. This feature added further character to the oddball light. A fixed, catoptric Fresnel lens with flashes supplied by electric lamps and an array of electronic foghorns complete the picture of automation. Red Rock is an unusual Canadian lighthouse, built in a difficult location and worthy of its engineers.

Lonely Island

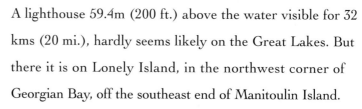

A lighthouse 59.4m (200 ft.) above the water visible for 32 kms (20 mi.), hardly seems likely on the Great Lakes. But there it is on Lonely Island, in the northwest corner of Georgian Bay, off the southeast end of Manitoulin Island.

First built on the north point of the island in 1870, a combined residence and tower topped the limestone bluffs, 40m (125 ft.) above the beach. Fire destroyed it in 1907, and a new, octagonal, wooden tower was placed on the same bluff site. The residence and other buildings were built on beach level, with pathway and stairs connecting them to the tower. My first visit in 1979 became an unexpected adventure when the keeper mysteriously equipped us with sticks. As we started up the path and the 100 steps to the tower, he leashed his dogs. Once on the bluff, we saw carefully-mowed pathways leading to and around the tower. We were warned not to stray from them. The whole place, we were told, was crawling with Mississauga rattlesnakes.

Lonely's tower is classic early 20th century. It is a tapering, white, wooden, octagon. Because the tower is squat, the standard platform and domed lamphouse seem large. The Chance Brothers lamphouse has a solid base, three tiers of windows, a smooth, round dome, and a large round ventilation cap topped with an "arrows and feathers" weather vane. It is a substantial and handsome light, and illustrates the principle that lighthouses built on high locations can light up the waters for great distances with comparatively short towers.

Lonely was built early in the era of frequent wrecks. When *Asia* disappeared with only two survivors from her 120 passengers and crew in an 1882 storm, interest in lighthouses grew intense. At Lonely light station, bodies from *Asia* began to drift ashore. A scandal was sparked when keeper Dominic Solomon was accused of lifting valuables before burying the dead. Flotsam appeared along the shore, such as doors, chairs, and bits of baggage. The exact location of *Asia's* foundering has never been discovered, but it must have been in the hurricane-roused seas east of Lonely.

Today the lumber trade is gone. Lonely looks out over vastly quietened waters. Passenger traffic—so vital in the early 1900s before many roads—is a trickle of pleasure craft and the occasional ferry. The station was de-staffed in 1986 after the departure of keeper Gibson, and converted to solar power the following year. A lightweight lens system and efficient, electric lamps were installed in the early 1990s. The beautiful 3rd Order Fresnel lens—so prominent in the picture—was dismantled and removed. The beachside station was largely razed in 1995. Lonely's trails and gardens have grown over, the stairs are in decay and the rattlesnakes are mostly undisturbed.

Great Duck Island

Dozens of variations of "Duck Island" show up on Canadian maps, a testament to the significance of the duck in the days of exploration. Farewell Duck Island is on the north coast of Newfoundland, False Ducks Island and Main Duck Island are near Kingston, Ontario and here, south of the western end of Manitoulin Island, we have Outer Duck, Middle Duck, Western Duck, and the largest of them all, Great Duck Island. Great Duck is situated along the main shipping routes across northern Lake Huron, making it an important lighthouse site.

The first lighthouse was built in 1877 on the southwestern end of Great Duck Island. Its design—a square pyramidal tower and attached keeper's quarters—was common at the time. Built of wood, it was more than 16m (50 ft.) high and topped with a polygonal lamphouse large enough to house ten burners with reflectors on a rotating frame. A steam-operated fog siren was installed a few years after the light and was replaced by a diaphone a few years later. When I first visited Great Duck in 1980, the diaphone had been replaced by electronic horns. But as Keeper Joe Thibeault demonstrated—to the enormous surprise of an unsuspecting helicopter crew resting nearby—the old diaphone was still in working order.

The modern tower was built in 1918 and, in 1980, it still had its 3rd Order Fresnel lens, which by then had been electrified. With automation, the station has been largely dismantled, its slender, 27m (90 ft.) tower attended by little more than small control houses, the electric fog alarm, and solar panels.

At the turn of the century, the first keeper on Great Duck, William Purvis, started a fishing industry with four of his sons. It blossomed and spread to other places in the area. The beach below the light is a wonderful display of pebbles and cobbles in a variety of colours and textures. These are Canadian Shield rocks, deposited by the south-moving icecap that covered all of this area, and which actually caused the Great Lakes to form.

LAKE SUPERIOR

Thunder Bay, Ontario

Gros Cap Crib

Officially called Gros Cap Reefs, the local name "Crib" refers to the location of the light: on a concrete crib in shallow water at the southwest extremity of the Gros Cap Reefs, in the entrance to the St. Mary's River, west of Sault Ste. Marie. The present structure, built in 1953, is a white, square tower with a V-point facing the drifting ice and waves of Lake Superior. It holds its flashing, white light 13.5m (45 ft.) above water level. A prominent helicopter landing pad attached at roof level is a sign of the times, as is a tall, radio mast. Electricity is supplied from the mainland via an underwater cable, and, as the boarded up windows suggest, the station is entirely automated and unstaffed. The site is accessible only by water. From here, the lighthouse station at Ile Parisienne is visible on clear days on the horizon to the north.

Gros Cap began as a lightship, 1927.

Ile Parisienne

At the southeast end of Lake Superior is Whitefish Bay, which flows into the St. Marys River. The Bay is split by the border between Canada and the United States. In the middle of the Bay, on the Canadian side, lies the north-south trending Ile Parisienne, about 10 kms (6 mi.) long, and wooded with sand and gravel shores. The main channel for shipping passes just to the west. The lighthouse station, built in 1912 on the south end of the island, is visible in the channel from each direction and marks the way in and out of the St. Marys River. This is a beautiful station with its red roofed, gleaming white buildings intact on a sand and gravel spit, backed by the wooded island and facing westward to Lake Superior, the great inland sea.

The 15m (48 ft.) tower is typical of those built at the time, at medium-sized stations all over Canada. It has a hexagonal, reinforced-concrete core and joined buttresses, which flare out at the top to form the supports for the platform. Its ten-sided lanternhouse is capped by a conical dome with a rare, distinctive beaver weather vane, like the one on far away Belle Isle (North), Newfoundland, which was built around the same time. The lanternhouse was constructed to hold a Fresnel lens system. Today it houses a very small, modern unit that produces a one-second flash every ten seconds. A substantial, south-facing array of solar panels supplies the power. Ile Parisienne is accessible by water, but for small boats is quite a long way out on open water.

Caribou Island

This photograph (taken by Anderson), shows wooden concrete forms being built progressively upward as the tower grew.

In the first decade of the 20th century, Lt. Col. W.P. Anderson, Chief Engineer and a Commissioner of Lights, developed a new design in lighthouses that featured a reinforced concrete, central tower supported by buttresses which radiated outward. On many of these towers, the buttresses were directly attached to the central core and were more like ribs. But a few of Anderson's designs had flying buttresses. The flying buttress form was used in several places in Canada and immediately drew world-wide admiration. One of these towers was built on a low-lying satellite island off Caribou Island well out into Lake Superior, south of Michipicoten. To this day, it is one of the most beautiful lighthouses in Canada. With its base very close to water level, it raises its light 30.2m (100 ft.) above water level and is visible over much of central Lake Superior.

A lighthouse was first placed here in 1886 but was replaced in 1912 by the present magnificent structure, a hexagonal tower with six flying buttresses. The buttresses each rise from the base, join the tower at two places on the way up, and then flare out to form supports for the platform. The design delighted the international lighthouse community. Not only was it beautiful, but it also supplied the stability required by tall towers. There were no 100-foot cranes or ready-mix delivered to the site—this tower was built mainly by hand labour.

When it first started service, the Caribou Island light was equipped with a 1st Order Fresnel lens system inside a handsome 12-sided, red lamphouse, its metal frames holding 36 panes of light-house-quality glass. As usual in big lamphouses, it had a platform with a railing, and another, much narrower platform above it at light level to enable the keeper to clean the glass regularly. Red-painted ladders led from the first platform to the second, to the guttered, round dome, and still higher, to the cap on top.

Now, with complete automation and destaffing, the two-storey, duplex keepers' house has been removed. Power is supplied by solar panels and the light itself is an airport beacon searchlight system, with special sealed beams. This beautiful tower is visible as a white finger on the horizon from as much as 24 kms (15 mi.) away on a fine day. From close range, the small unit replacing the magnificent Fresnel lens makes it seem empty eyed. Nonetheless, the automated light still supplies a faithful beacon.

One event is of special note in its history. In November 1978, the *Edmund Fitzgerald*, the largest laker of that time, set sail in threatening weather from Superior, Wisconsin. She was bound for the east end of Lake Superior and beyond, heavily laden with iron ore. As the weather grew worse, the Captain elected to pass to the north in the lee of the Canadian shore and then turn southward for the Sault. They sailed with another ship past the end of Michipicoten Island and southward in the night beyond Caribou Island. But then, in the raging storm, the other ship suddenly lost radar contact with the *Fitzgerald*. Few traces of the huge ship or her crew were found in the calm morning seas. Even after divers had found and explored the wreck, the sudden end—without so much as a distress call—was never sufficiently explained. The Caribou Island light may have been the final human contact for her crew.

Caribou Island is only accessible by air or by water but is a long way out for small boats on open waters. Even so, this beautiful station is a national treasure and should be given top priority for preservation.

Davieaux Island

A series of rocky islands lies south of Quebec Harbour, about halfway along the south shore of Michipicoten Island in the northeast corner of Lake Superior. In 1872, a lighthouse was placed on the summit of the largest, Davieaux Island. The station is unique in that its light tower sits alone on a rocky summit, while the keepers' houses are situated lower and to the east. The old power and service buildings are further east. The fog horns are even farther away on the end of the island. All automated and unstaffed now, the station runs on solar panels. A hundred years ago, ships needing help through fog would blow their horns and the keepers would hasten to sound their fog horns in reply. Today, in a throwback to that practice, the electronic horn at Davieaux sounds automatically when captains of passing vessels press their radio keys five times. It all happens remotely—and anonymously—in the fog.

Michipicoten Island

One of Colonel Anderson's lovely, flying buttress towers stands lonely vigil at the east end of
Michipicoten Island in the northest corner of Lake Superior. In days before automation, electronic
foghorns and solar cells, this station was the ideal Canadian light station. The beautiful tower
presided over its red-roofed houses, the boathouse and ramp, the power and fog horn buildings,
all backing on a steep hillside with thick woods. Southern views offered Superior's limitless horizon.
It must have been wonderful to live here with the offshore fishing, woods at the back door, and
archaeological sites and artifacts to give a sense of history.

Otter Island

Since 1903, Otter Island lighthouse has been a nighttime signpost on the north shore of Lake Superior, at the southern end of a long, rugged shoreline along the Pukaskwa peninsula. The island is now part of Pukaskwa National Park This wild stretch of Superior shoreline is a favourite of canoeists and kayakers with its occasional coves and sandy beaches tucked in amongst small islands. The light at Otter Island is a standard, concrete tower with red lamphouse. Its residences are set well back from the exposed shore that faces open water. Now automated, the station receives its power from solar cells.

Slate Islands

The rocky Slate Islands stand out from Lake Superior's north shore, about 40 kms (25 mi.) west of Marathon. A lighthouse station was built on their southern extremity in 1903—a beacon on this largely unoccupied stretch of rock bound coast. The station on the flat near the shoreline is now much reduced in automation. But the 10.4m (35 ft.), white tower still stands on its high rocky ridge 57m (180 ft.) above the water. Its red lanternhouse, capped by its beaver weather vane, still sends out its warning flash every 15 seconds.

Battle Island

In 1877, a lighthouse was built on the west end of Battle Island, marking the entrance to Nipigon Bay on the north shore of Lake Superior. The existing light sits atop a standard, white, octagonal tower 12m (40 ft.) high. Although it is completely automated, this station is largely intact. In 1998, it was occupied by a former keeper who preferred to live here more than anywhere else. Its remote location is accessible by boat but is a long way from anywhere.

Porphyry Point

A thousand miles inland from the sea, Thunder Bay is at the head of the Great Lakes/St. Lawrence waterway. It is guarded by a series of islands and peninsulas extending eastward along the north shore of Lake Superior. About 35 nautical miles east of Thunder Bay is Porphyry Island at the entrance to Black Bay. A light station was established here in 1873. When I visited in 1980, the lighthouse was a square tower with a lattice daymark all the way up to the platform and octagonal lamphouse. The old fog alarm building with flared horn pointing toward the water was still there with a bank of electronic horns beside it (see photo). With its 25m (80 ft.) tower and group of red-roofed service buildings, the station made a bright spot of colour on the lonely, dark coastline.

Trowbridge Island

The Trowbridge Island light is a beautiful station on the north side of the entrance to Thunder Bay at the west end of Lake Superior. The white, concrete 11.3-m (37-ft.) tower with red lanternhouse sits by itself on the summit of the wooded island. The red-roofed residence, fog horn and service buildings were built on separate spots, joined to each other and the summit by walkways and stairs. Because the top of the island is so high above water, the light from the short tower is visible for many miles on Lake Superior. Trowbridge offers the best of Lake Superior island scenery and a constant stream of shipping, lakers and "salties", passing by. The station has been automated and destaffed.

Pilot Point, B.C.

BRITISH COLUMBIA

The west coast of North America from Mexico to Alaska was explored by Spaniards in the 17th century, by Captain Cook in the 1770s and by Captain Vancouver in the 1780s. Many of the original names given to capes, islands and bays by these early adventurers endure today. Langara, Juan de Fuca, Estevan and Ballinas are Spanish in origin. Point Atkinson, Cape Flattery, and scores of others were named after British naval captains, their political friends, and their ships. Names also described the environs and how the captains felt about them, such as Race Rocks and Captain Cook's Friendly Cove.

The mountains meet the sea on this spectacular coast. Gouged and eroded by glaciers, the edge of the continent is deeply indented by fiords and long inlets, with a myriad of islands and reefs. Many harbours are excellent as at Vancouver and Victoria.

West-coast settlements began modestly in California in the early 1800s and at Victoria by 1820. When the gold rush came to California in 1849 so did a swarm of ships, rounding Cape Horn and coming up the west coast. For some time, whales and fur seals drew ships and settlers farther north. But the coasts were dark at night and the currents unknown. Winter gales smashed into the rocky shores and fogs obscured even the areas that were well known. There were many shipwrecks with heavy loss of life. After several months in unforgiving seas, how tragic to be torn apart on the rocks so near your destination.

In 1858, thousands of men with gold fever rushed up the Fraser River into Cariboo country. By that time, more than 500 vessels a year were landing at Victoria. Wrecks were too many to ignore. In 1852, the U.S. Congress authorized 16 lighthouses along the American coast, including one at Cape Flattery on the south side of the entrance to the Strait of Juan de Fuca. When it was lit in 1857, British and Canadian authorities felt pressure to reciprocate and protect their waters just to the north. Coming up the coast past Oregon and Washington, ships often met persistent, blinding fogs. Navigation had to be by "dead reckoning", meaning that the speed and direction of the ship in the water were measured, the time noted, and a position plotted. The trouble with navigating in this way was that the movement of ocean currents was not known and along the west coast various currents set vessels well to the north of where they thought they were. They turned in towards Juan de Fuca in the fog or dark of night only to end up with breakers ahead on the rock-strewn, lee shore of the western side of Vancouver Island. Even if they had seen Cape Flattery light there was nothing beyond to bracket the entrance to the bay.

The situation had become intolerable and so the Royal Navy prepared a survey for the British Admiralty, naming Race Rocks and Fisgard Island as places to light the approaches to Victoria and beyond. In London, a Captain Sulivan championed the lighthouse cause. Twenty years earlier he had served on H.M.S. *Beagle* with a young naturalist, Charles Darwin, with whom Sulivan had a close association. Darwin's observations on that four-year voyage revolutionized natural science, establishing the voyage as one of the great scientific epics of all time.

Lit in 1860, Race Rocks and Fisgard began an era of lighthouse building in British Columbia, initiated in part by local authorities and by the British Admiralty. Canada took over in 1871 when British Columbia joined Confederation. By the early 1900s, dozens of lights marked the hazardous outside coast of Vancouver Island and the Inside Passage. Activity on the Inside Passage was stimulated by gold discovered in 1898 on the Klondike. Shipwreck and tragedy continued, however, well into the 20th century and many lights owe their existence to major shipwrecks. Today wrecks are rare now that radar and satellite position indicators are in common use, and marine traffic control covers most of the coasts.

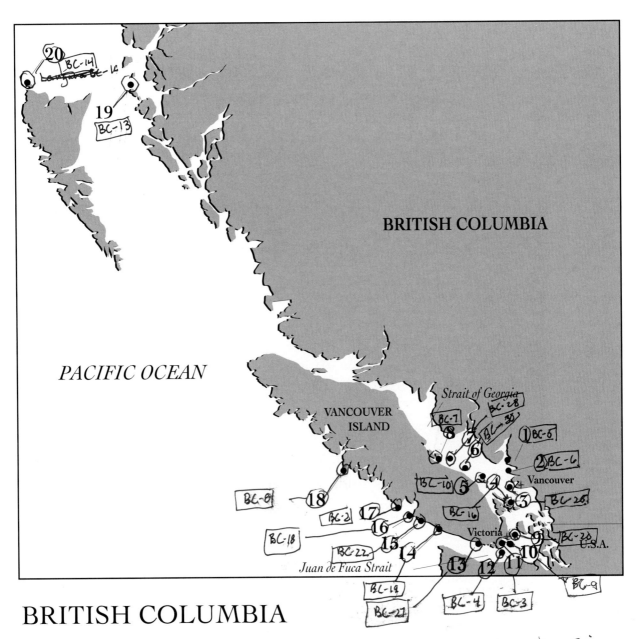

PACIFIC OCEAN

BRITISH COLUMBIA

VANCOUVER ISLAND

Strait of Georgia

Vancouver

Victoria

Juan de Fuca Strait

U.S.A.

Pilot Point - BC-1

BRITISH COLUMBIA

1. Brockton Point BC-5
2. Point Atkinson BC-6
3. Sand Heads BC-25
4. Active Pass BC-16
5. Entrance Island BC-10
6. Ballenas Island BC-30
7. Sisters BC-28
8. Chrome Island BC-7
9. Discovery Island BC-20
10. Trial Island BC-9

11. Fisgard BC-3
12. Race Rocks BC-4
13. Sheringham Point BC-27
14. Carmanah BC-19
15. Pachena Point BC-22
16. Cape Beale BC-18
17. Amphitrite BC-2
18. Estevan Point BC-8
19. Triple Island BC-13
20. Langara BC-14

VANCOUVER &
STRAITS of GEORGIA

Cape Mudge, British Columbia

Brockton Point

Poised on a point in Stanley Park—in the middle of the city of Vancouver—it is hard to take Brockton Point seriously as an aid to navigation. Yet, in 1890, a temporary light was needed there to complement the Prospect Point light around the corner. Together they would serve ships looking for the harbour mouth. The first keeper, Captain William Jones, was an interesting character. He started out at Brockton by building his own shanty house out of driftwood. Later, an official house was built with the light shining out an upper dormer window. Jones was also a gardener and at one time his income from the sale of his flowers matched his earnings as keeper.

Ships coming and going through the narrows were blind to one another. Brockton therefore established a signalling system with Prospect Point. Despite these precautions, ships continued to be lost in the narrows. In 1914, Col. Anderson, Chief Engineer of the Lighthouse Board, designed a new light, especially for Brockton. It was a solid, square concrete box atop arches over the shore walkway. Walkers, joggers, bicyclists and visitors use the now-automated tower as a landmark. The look-out offers a view of one of the busiest and most beautiful harbours in the world. Ferries and tugboats bustle back and forth. Long bulk carriers tie up at the docks opposite and load sulphur and wood chips. Cruise ships, their railings lined with passengers, dock at this "foreign port". And countless pleasure boats attend to the serious business of having a good time.

This is probably the most easily accessible lighthouse in Canada. Drive through Stanley Park in downtown Vancouver to a parking lot in front of the lighthouse. It is also one of the most interesting lights to visit, not so much for its technical wonders as for its lively seaport and magnificent scenery.

Point Atkinson

On a Sunday morning in 1980, I decided to try to arrange a visit to Point Atkinson lighthouse. There was a pause in the convention I was attending in Vancouver, and I was intrigued by pictures showing this famous light on an isolated, wooded point, seemingly far from the city. A brief inquiry at the desk of my hotel yielded specific directions: "Sure, step across the street to the bus stop, take #23 and when the driver announces "Lighthouse", get off." Sure enough, the bus stopped a half hour later. I followed a well-marked park trail through the west-coast rain forest and there it was, one of Col. Anderson's six sided, buttressed, concrete light towers.

It wasn't that easy when the first wooden lighthouse was built here in 1874. On the north side of the entrance to Burrard Bay, 11 kms (7 mi.) from where the Lion's Gate Bridge now stands, the isolation was too much for the first keeper's family. The next keeper, Erwin, arrived in 1880 and stayed for 30 years, becoming a part of the legend of that coast and of the community that grew slowly nearby. In 1890, a siren-type fog alarm was installed and was replaced by a powerful diaphone in 1902. The steam-drive diaphone required significantly more labour and vigilance from the keeper, what with lugging coal, stoking, cleaning, and general maintenance. Erwin hired a helper, Thomas Grafton, who succeeded him two decades later and kept the light for 20 more years. Grafton's forty-year tenure is one of the longest in Canadian lighthouse history. It ended one morning in 1933 as he was "fishing" for his breakfast in front of the light, and the dynamite he was using accidentally misfired.

In these days, while the debate rages about staffed versus automated lighthouses, I recall the assistant keeper that Sunday afternoon, diligently scanning the broad reaches of Burrard Bay with its hundreds of pleasure boats dotting the blue surface. His job was to watch for upsets and collisions and to call for help when needed, a service beyond the means of radar or computers.

Sand Heads

The many branches of the Fraser River delta are characterized by shifting channels, shallow water, and alluvial sediment. Lightships were used to mark the main channel for shipping until 1957, when a light station was built on piles driven into the bottom. By 1998, the old platform had deteriorated and was slated for replacement in some form. Unstaffed and automated, it remains Canada's only major light built on pilings in this way.

Active Pass

Hundreds of thousands of passengers lean on the railings of the Tsawwassen-Victoria ferries every year as they pass through the narrow channel of Active Pass between Mayne (south side) and Galiano Islands. Before them is the slim tower of the Active Pass light station with its flashing light and red-roofed buildings. These days, the powerful ferries plough through the pass regardless of the tides and currents, slowing only in the narrower portions and sounding their horns to warn other traffic. It was not always so. Sailing ships encountered the hazards of swirling currents and tide rips in a narrow, high-walled passage. Wrecks were frequent and still occur. The S.S. *Princess Adelaide* grounded right in front on the light station in 1918. (She was later refloated without further complications.)

When the first light was built at Active Pass in 1885, it was a fixed, white, kerosene light. It was replaced in 1910 by an occulting, white, vapour lamp and, in 1928, by an electric bulb with reflector mirror. After several more adjustments, a circular, concrete tower was built in 1969, separate from the residence. It now supports a rotating airport-type beacon shining a steady, white light, with superimposed flash every ten seconds. Active Pass station has an aero-marine radio beacon and in addition to lightkeeping duties, the keeper makes weather reports, and records seawater temperature and salinity.

The first keeper was Henry "Scotty" Georgeson, a Shetland Islander who had a varied career in pioneer British Columbia before taking up a career on lights. He stayed at Active Pass for 36 years, before retiring in 1921 at the age of 85. His brother James also emigrated and became the keeper of the East Point (Saturna) light in 1889. No fewer than eight family members of these two Georgesons were lightkeepers in the southern Gulf Islands.

Entrance Island

For passengers on the Nanaimo-Horseshoe Bay ferry, Entrance Island lighthouse appears to the south of Nanaimo on a low, rocky island, set against the wooded shore of Gabriola Island. In 1870, a year after a major coal-mining operation began in the Nanaimo district, dozens of ships laden with coal sailed for Pacific ports. Unlike the outside lights built in the wake of major wrecks and loss of life, this light station was built out of local pride and convenience.

In 1875, Entrance Island light began service with the usual three-story, wooden light tower on the corner of a two-story residence. Both lamp and lens were progressively upgraded until 1921 when a Chance-built, fourth order revolving lens was installed in a mercury-float chamber. A steam foghorn was installed in 1894 requiring the added burden of lugging coal and firing up the boilers to raise the steam. The keeper was relieved of these duties in 1915 when gasoline engines were used to compress air to drive the diaphone. The fog alarm was updated to an electronic signal system in 1971. The *List of Lights* records the slender, modern, concrete tower as 10.7m (36 ft.) high and the light at 18.6m (62 ft.) above the sea. Entrance Island is still staffed although most functions are automated. This bare rock near the lovely, settled Gabriola Island is only accessible by boat.

Ballenas Island

Named by exploring Spaniards in 1794, the Ballenas Islands are out from Parksville on the eastern side of Vancouver Island. Here again, a light was built to serve the increasing traffic on that part of the Inside Passage. Plans for the station were drawn in 1899, but there was confusion about the location. On a high point on South Ballenas Island, construction proceeded on a standard, rectangular building with a square lantern on the roof. Its fixed light was visible for more than 16 kms (10 mi.). Despite its range, the light was hard to see from the shipping channels. Shipowners brought pressure to bear on Ottawa, and in 1906, the government ordered the light moved to a better location. Finally, in 1912, the station was rebuilt on a rocky point on North Ballenas Island. The station has been upgraded several times and is now a white, octagonal concrete tower 11.3m (38 ft.) high. Its light is 21.3m (71 ft.) above the water. A diaphone was installed in 1908 and updated in 1968. Now automated and unstaffed, the station remains largely intact.

Sisters Rocks

By 1897, traffic along the Inside Passage was increasing rapidly with the lure of Alaskan gold and the new settlements to the north. With narrow channels between rocky islands, and complex, violent tidal currents, placing lights here became vital. In 1898, stations were established at Cape Mudge, opposite Campbell River, and on the Sisters Rocks to the south in more open water. The latter is a group of very small rocks, the highest of which stands only 5.1m (17 ft.) above high tide. A wooden structure with light tower was built on a massive concrete pad, with smaller service buildings crowded nearby. It showed a fixed light.

From the first, the Sisters was a miserable station with a succession of disgruntled keepers who stayed only a few months. It was less than an acre of bare rock, wave-washed in every storm, and inaccessible for long periods in the winter months. Its house and tower were both badly built and leaky. It was rebuilt in 1967 with a much more solid base for living quarters, engine house and fog alarm. A slender, concrete tower was constructed for the modern light. The 1908 diaphone fog alarm was converted to the electronic style in 1968. No longer staffed, the station is boarded up, and runs automatically.

Chrome Island

BC - 7

On January 1,1891, a light was first lit on Yellow Island, just off the southern tip of Denman Island, and south of Courtney. Ships carrying coal from Union Bay and other points along the shore required use of Baynes Sound, and this little island (now called Chrome Island) at the southern entrance to the Sound was the spot chosen for a lighthouse. The first light was fixed on the roof of the keeper's residence. In 1922, a new light in a small wooden cupola was installed high on steel legs. A rotating beacon and new residences followed in 1929, and a new, circular, concrete tower came on line in the early 1980s. The tower flared out to a platform, holding a lamphouse with eight, inward sloping, rectangular glass panes. By that time, the station was already running on electricity with power from Denman Island.

What sets Chrome Island apart from all other stations is the Stone Age petroglyphs visible on its rock surfaces. Many have been destroyed over the years by the construction of the station, subsequent alterations, visitors, and the sea birds—principally cormorants in noisy numbers—occupying the cliffs.

Chrome Island light is accessible by boat. The nearby wreck of the *Alpha* in late 1900 provides a favoured diving site. *Alpha's* anchor, recovered on a diving expedition in 1972, now lies near the ferry dock on Denman Island. Chrome is automated and in 1999 is still staffed. It is quite a sight from the water against the backdrop of wooded islands and the mountains of Vancouver Island.

VANCOUVER
ISLAND

BC-9

Trial Island, British Columbia

BC-20

Discovery Island

If you've dreamed about lightkeeping, Discovery station—on a wooded island about 8 kms (5 mi.) east of Victoria—would have been just the spot. The climate is pleasant, and getting there is easy by small boat. Lying astride the southeastern entrance to the Strait of Georgia, it overlooks a steady stream of shipping from all over the world. Beyond the seascapes, distant mountains frame the view in all directions. When I first landed here, the assistant keeper was busy mowing the lawn. We began to chat and he told me that having grown tired of his job as an Ontario Provincial Police officer, he had come west to the calm of the lighthouse service.

Like so many Canadian coastal features, Discovery Island was named after a Royal Navy exploring ship, H.M.S. *Discovery*, that sailed here in 1784 under Captain Vancouver. The original station was built in 1886 in the fashion of the time: a wood, three-storey tower with a round, Chance Brothers lamphouse, all in a single unit with the two-storey residence.

From 1871, when British Columbia joined Confederation, until the Second World War, lightkeepers were appointed based on unadulterated patronage. One of the worst examples was the 1884 appointment of Richard Brinn as the first keeper on Discovery. Incompetent and ill from the start, his daughter, Mary Ann Croft, covered for him and was de facto keeper for more than a decade. When Brinn finally died in 1901, the bureaucracy fumbled about, hesitant about hiring a woman, but common sense finally prevailed and Mary Ann Croft was named his successor. During her 30 years of service, Mary Ann Croft was recognized as an excellent keeper, and in 1934, was presented with the Imperial Service Medal.

Originally, a fog alarm bell was housed in a separate structure on the waterside until 1893 when it was replaced by a louder steam alarm plant. The early square, wooden tower was replaced by the existing, slender concrete tower in 1978.

Trial Island

Weekend crowds in Victoria descend on Marine Drive, from Clover Point to Gonzales Park. They walk the beaches, feed the gulls and pigeons and look out across the sea at the Olympic mountains in Washington. Just in front of them is a bare rocky island separated at its closest point by 100m (320 ft.) of water. At its farthest point are the radio towers and slender white column of Trial Island light station, white sentinel by day, flashing light by night. It is a serious hazard to attempt the narrow channel, for rip currents surge between the rocks at up to eight knots.

By the end of the century, it was clear that a light with a foghorn on the outer end of Trial Island would be of great use to shipping. In 1905, construction began on a two-story, wooden building with a light tower at the four-way central peak, as was customary at that time. With lots of rain on the rocky island, a large cistern was part of the design. A temporary, fixed light shone in late 1906, replaced a short time later by a rotating, Chance Brothers, Fresnel lens system of the Third Order.

A diaphone fog horn was part of the original installation and boomed out across the foggy strait until 1970 when it was replaced by an electronic horn. In the same year, the existing tower with a rotating bull's-eye light was installed. The original lamphouse and lens were carefully dismantled and reconstructed in Bastion Square in downtown Victoria, where it looks out over a different kind of traffic.

Fisgard Island

Work on Fisgard Island light began in 1859, soon after the site was chosen by two Royal Navy captains, Richards of H.M.S. *Pumper* and Fulford of H.M.S. *Ganges*. They had also designated Race Rocks as a lighthouse site, set for immediate construction. A spot on the rocky knob of Fisgard was levelled and a foundation course of solid granite blocks was laid. The tower and keeper's quarters were made of brick. The tower walls were 1.2m (4 ft.) thick at the base tapering to a collar of decorative brickwork beneath the platform. A beautiful spiral staircase, cast in San Francisco, was installed. Within a few years, the brickwork began to deteriorate and so in 1872-73, the tower was coated in cement and thickly painted.

Distinguishing it from American fixed lights on the nearby coast, this light was made to revolve with weights and clockwork. Its coloured glass panels—used to give different coloured flashes— had been broken during construction, and it took most of a year to replace them. Listed as having begun service in 1860, it was likely not until 1863 or 1864 that all the glass panes were installed. Its illumination history was fairly standard: wick lamps burned a succession of fuels—colza oil, then shark's oil from local sources and, in 1890, kerosene—behind a Chance Brothers dioptric lens system. Since 1928, it has been an automated electric sector light.

Fisgard light, along with the old Fort Rudd beside it, is now part of a National Historic Site and Park, and is easily accessible by road from Victoria. A causeway joins it to the mainland and each year, visitors in the thousands walk out onto this former island, admiring the view and the passings ships. Historical exhibits oddly featuring numerous wrecks fill the lovely old tower and residence.

Race Rocks

One of Canada's greatest lighthouses was built on Race Rocks. Set on the largest island astride the main channel on the north side of the Juan de Fuca Strait, it is located ten nautical miles down the coast from Fisgard towards the open sea. The heavy tide around the rocks—hence the name—set ships off course in weather fair or foul. Even after the light was active, sailing ships wound up on its rocky ledges.

Blocks of stone for this tower were cut in Scotland, fitted and numbered, then shipped around Cape Horn as ballast in sailing ships. At Race Rocks, they were unloaded when weather and tides allowed, and hauled up to the site. The rather beautiful "built by number" tower remains in service to this day. The light has always revolved, first beamed out from simple reflectors, and later from Chance Brothers' best dioptric lens. At the time of my first visit, in 1982, the light source was provided by banks of four sealed beam lights on rotating panels.

Among the dozens of Race Rocks wrecks, one of the most horrifying was that of a very small boat bringing the brother of the keeper's wife and three others for Christmas in 1865. Ten metres from shore, a sharp change in currents caught the laden boat, capsized it, throwing everything—people, presents and supplies—into the water, right in front of the keeper and his wife who were on the landing to greet them. Nothing could save the visitors from the fierce currents and all were drowned.

On March 24, 1911, with a full gale blowing, the ferry *Sechelt* departed Victoria for Sooke, just down the coast. The captain decided to turn back near Race Rocks, but as *Sechelt* came beam to the wind, she capsized and nearly a hundred were lost. Victoria newspapers of the late 19th and early 20th centuries had repeated accounts of shipwrecks in these dangerous waters.

A fog bell was installed very early on Race Rocks, and was replaced by a much louder foghorn in 1892. When wrecks continued, some surviving crews complained that the fog alarm had not been working. The mystery deepened as investigations showed that the fog horn had been blasting all the time. Desperate to provide a reliable alert, authorities installed the first radio beacon in Canadian lights on Race Rock in July 1927. But what was wrong with the fog horn?

A careful study in 1929 showed a significant "silent zone" where the sound was deflected by buildings and topography, silencing the horn. Moving the horn a short distance from the tower cured the situation. (Over the years, the "silent zone" problem has frequently occurred. When the big low notes of the diaphones were replaced by the higher-pitched squeals of electronic horns, silent zones appeared at lights such as Cape St. Mary's in Newfoundland.)

Today Race Rocks is automated and unstaffed. The grounds and residence are cared for by nearby Pearson College which offers summer programs at the site (see photo p.31).

Sheringham Point

A light station was put on Sheringham Point in 1912 for coastwise shipping and traffic along the Strait of Juan de Fuca. This light helped fill the 80-km (50-mi.) gap between Race Rocks, to the southeast, and Carmanah, along the coast to the northwest. The point was named in 1842 after Royal Navy Admiral Sheringham although it had already been named Punta de San Eusivio by Spanish navigators in 1790.

Its original, white, hexagonal, concrete tower (19.5m or 65 ft. high) sits on a rocky point close to the water. Its modest buttresses flare out under the light platform that supports the round, Chance Brothers lantern housing. In 1976, the original 3rd Order Fresnel lens was replaced with a revolving searchlight-style lamp. A horn was installed in 1925 and replaced with an electronic one in 1976.

Unlike the more remote stations northwest along the coast, fishing boats and some sea-going pleasure craft pass by in a steady stream. Naval gunfire is occasionally heard from a nearby gunnery range. All of the support buildings are gone, leaving an austere, automated station. It is easy to get there, though, as it is just off the main coastal road west and north from Victoria.

Carmanah

By the mid-19th century, several hundred ships a year were coming into Victoria and marine traffic was increasing all the time. As the ships came in looking for a landfall, they would encounter a foggy, stormy coastline for several months a year. In 1870 there were still no lights north of Cape Flattery, Washington. (Race Rocks and Fisgard (both 1860) were well in the Strait of Juan de Fuca towards Victoria.) The rest of Vancouver Island's outer coast was dark. Cape Beale light was in operation by 1874, but that still left a long, dark gap where wrecks continued to claim ships, hundreds of people and tons of cargo.

As ships came up the coast, knowing when to turn east into the Strait of Juan de Fuca was not easy, especially during winter nights, dense fogs and gales. Thinking they had found the right place to enter, ships would commonly meet the jagged rocks of the B.C. coast, instead of the open strait. To help solve the problem, a site was chosen on Bonilla Point. Lighthouse folklore tells how the construction crew came ashore in the fog, hauled supplies and construction materials up the cliffs and, when the fog cleared later, did not find themselves on Bonilla Pt. but on the neighbouring Carmanah Point. It was just as good a spot, so they built the lighthouse there. Carmanah light first sent out its powerful beams in September 1891. With its telegraph line to Victoria and a system of "speaking" to ships by flag signals, it soon became the communications centre for B.C. coastal traffic.

The original Carmanah light was the standard, square, wooden tower, a Chance Brothers lantern and lens on top, and the keeper's house attached. It was 14m (46 ft.) high but its position on the headland gave it a height of more than 51m (170 ft.) above water, making its beam visible for 19 nautical miles on a clear night. The light is a concrete tower with flaring platform, red lantern house and 3rd Order Chance Brothers lens system. Replacement of the beautiful old glass lenses is proceeding and even the lens at Pachena, now a National Historic Site, has gone. The tower and service buildings in white with red roofs make a pleasant compound there on the edge of the cliffs, backed by the heavy west coast rain forests. Carmanah light can be seen along the West Coast Trail that skirts the rocky cliffs of this coast. Now a popular hiking trail, it was originally established to facilitate rescue of the hundreds of mariners who have been stranded or perished on the rocks and shoals of this dangerous coast.

Carmanah, B.C.

Pachena Point

Just as traffic signals are installed when someone is killed at an intersection, so it has often been with lighthouses. Pachena Point lighthouse is an example. Carmanah helped avert many disasters once it was built in 1891, but the toll in lives and ships continued to mount.

On January 22, 1906, *Valencia*, set out from San Francisco on her routine run to Victoria. Having made the trip many times before, Captain Johnson set out confidently with 134 passengers and crew aboard. *Valencia* encountered fog almost at once. For the next 54 hours, Captain Johnson groped his way blindly northward. His calculations told him it was time to adjust course to enter the Strait of Juan de Fuca.

The Captain became increasingly alarmed as nothing seemed to fit the soundings on his charts. The wind, waves and currents had set *Valencia* some 80 kms (50 mi.) north of where the Captain thought he was. Through the fog the dark shapes of rocks and cliffs suddenly appeared. Johnson made a frantic change of course to get back out into deep water, but it was too late — *Valencia* was hard aground.

Despite the crashing surf, a lifeboat was filled and launched. It was soon dashed to pieces with all hands lost. Hours passed. A few passengers had stumbled ashore from a raft and found the telegraph trail. Soon the word was out. Ships arrived offshore but could not get close in the heavy seas.

Towards the end, passengers clung together as *Valencia* settled deeper into the sea. Desperate to survive, some crawled into the rigging, but soon exhausted, they dropped into the breaking waves. Just four days after her departure from the docks of San Francisco, *Valencia's* broken hulk slid below the waves. The bodies of 117 passengers and crew littered the shore or drifted in the deep. The seventeen survivors and the witnesses described the scene to the press. Public outrage mounted in both Canada and the U.S.

Many tragic wrecks like *Valencia* have taken place on Canadian shores — Cape Race, St. Paul's Island, N.S., but few have garnered such attention. After *Valencia*, Ottawa appointed a commission that recommended the construction of a lighthouse at Pachena, and another at Sheringham Point.

A memorial to *Valencia*, the beautiful, hexagonal, wooden, shingled tower still stands atop the cliff at Pachena. The classic Chance Brothers lanternhouse, with its curved sheets of glass, was erected on the platform and its First Order Fresnel lens installed. It went into service on the clear night of May 21, 1907, and its flash was even observed on the American side of the Strait, 28 nautical miles away. It would be nice to report an end to wrecks along that shore, now protected by overlapping lights from Carmanah to Cape Beale. However, ships continued to misjudge the turn into the Strait. *Soquel* was wrecked near Pachena in January 1909, but that time keeper Erwin was able to alert help, and all hands were saved.

Now this beautiful lighthouse is preserved as a National Historical Site. Its great lens is gone, but a powerful searchlight sends its million-candlepower beam out to sea.

Cape Beale

When British Columbia joined Confederation in 1871, Prime Minister John A. Macdonald promised a railway to link the west coast with the rest of Canada and fulfill the National Dream. Excited by the prospect of increased trade and profit, business interests on Vancouver Island pictured Victoria—already a bustling port—as the new commercial gateway to the west coast. Others thought the railway might cross the Georgia Strait to Vancouver Island farther north, perhaps ending at Barkley Sound, on the outside coast. For ships at the time, this would have shaved two or three days off the Canadian Pacific Trans-Pacific route.

Thus it was easy to justify a lighthouse at Cape Beale, at the entrance to Barkley Sound. Not only would it mark the passage but it would also be a landfall light for the west coast, which at the time was dark along so much of its length. Bad weather and unfamiliarity with the coast made the first surveyors turn back in late 1872. They tried again in the summer of 1873 and approved the site. The short, stubby tower, just 10m (33 ft.) high, was completed that summer and the light put into service July 1, 1874. The first keeper stayed only until 1877 when the isolation got to be too much for his family. His successor, Emmanuel Cox, his wife Frances and their five children, became an outstanding lighthouse family.

Cape Beale's history is full of wrecks and bravery, family troubles and frustrating struggles with bureaucrats for supplies and services. But it was the wreck of *Coloma*, in the wintry seas of 1906, that drew world attention to this remote station.

Keeper Tom Patterson felt it in his bones that a gale was brewing. Soon the winds were howling on the Cape at 80 knots, and giant waves pounded the shore. In the first light of day, Patterson spotted a battered sailing ship offshore, her decks swept clean of everything, including lifeboats. He knew that the black specks on the rigging were crew members clinging for their lives. The telegraph line to Bamfield, undependable at best, had been snapped by fallen trees. He and his wife Minnie decided that he would go down to the nearest point on the rocks to see if he could help and she would try to get to Bamfield.

Minnie struggled through the tangled, sodden forest for hours and with local help rowed out through the slanting rain to the anchored *Quadra*. The captain immediately put out to sea. Minnie was exhausted but anxious to return to her nursing baby. Operators from the cable station rowed her down the shore.

Quadra managed to reach the foundering *Coloma*, launch a rescue boat and save the crew, just before she went to pieces on the reef. Once word of her heroic trek had reached the press, Minnie Patterson became an overnight sensation. Interviews and gifts, medals and cash just enhanced her public image as a wonderfully modest heroine.

Amphitrite Point

Amphitrite Point Light is another West Coast light that owes its presence to the death of a ship. *Pass of Melfort* was a sorry sight. In 1905, she had been anchored for weeks in Panama waiting for cargo when her captain decided to sail north to Puget Sound to load lumber.

Rocks at Amphitrite

It was now late December, and a tremendous gale swept the west coast making sailing hazardous for wind-driven ships. At Ucluelet, local Indians reported seeing rockets on Christmas Eve, and a search party was assembled. The next day, searchers found masses of wreckage— some identifiable as *Pass of Melfort*—

Daily Colonist.

(ESTABLISHED 1858.)

VICTORIA. B. C. FRIDAY, DECEMBER 29, 1905.

HAI
WELLING

ıshing
Out Revolt

w Officials Claim to Have
he Situation Well-In
Hand.

Spreading in Poland and
eparations Made for
Rising.

hat the Recent Issue of
ds May Presage Finen-
cial Crash.

VICTIMS OF WRECK
BURIED AT UCLUELET

Without Benefit of Clergy Bodies Washed Ashore Are
Laid Away While Villagers Knelt to Pray for Souls
of Dead Seamen--Twenty-Five Victims--Captain's Wife
Believed To Be Among the Dead--Siwashes Tell of Firing of Rockets During Last Hours. of Pass of Melfort.

and battered bodies washing ashore. There was a debate about the absence of lights. No one could say for sure if a lighthouse would have saved the *Pass of Melfort* that wild night, but the principle was strong. A temporary, wooden structure with a long-burning wick light was put on Amphitrite Point in 1906. It functioned until January 1914, when a tsunami (tidal wave) swept the site clean. Action to replace the light was fairly swift and, by the next spring, a squat, square, blocky concrete "tower" with light on top had been built, strange to the eye but obviously solid. It has operated through to the present day.

The lighthouse is easy to reach by road from Ucluelet and thousands of Pacific Rim National Park visitors come here every year. Just above the light is a modern building where a team of skilled technicians keeps track of shipping within an 80-km (50-mi.) radius. They work closely with a similar station in Washington State to direct traffic on that strategic portion of coast. Next to the traffic controllers is a bank of radar screens, and experts who coordinate rescue when emergencies arise in the eastern Pacific... a vast improvement from days of the hapless *Pass of Melfort* nearly a century ago.

Estevan Point

In the early 1900s, Col. William Anderson was engineer in charge of construction and Chairman of the Lighthouse Board of Canada. He was under continuing pressure to extend the lighthouse system north along the outside coast of Vancouver Island. Mindful of his own inspection trips along that coast, he chose Estevan Point on the Hesquiat Peninsula for a new light.

Estevan Light began service in 1910. Its design was one of the best from this celebrated lighthouse engineer. It still stands as one of the most beautiful lighthouses in Canada. There are similar Anderson designs at Caribou Island light in Lake Superior (1912), and Father Point (Point au Père) on the St. Lawrence (1909).

Anderson's brilliant design soon became known all over the world, not only for its beautiful shape but also for the stability its buttresses provided the tower. Anderson built smaller versions at Michipicoten Island in Lake Superior (1912), and at Belle Isle North, Nfld., where an outer casing

with flying buttresses was added to an earlier tower. More common among Anderson designs are the octagonal towers with fixed buttresses at the corners, as seen at Point Atkinson and Sheringham.

It was difficult to build at Estevan as that rocky coast was continuously wet and often stormy. A landing place was picked around the corner near the Indian village of Hesquiat and a tramway built 8 kms (5 mi.) through the woods to the site. All the materials had to come over that route: tons of sand and gravel; hundreds of bags of cement; lumber for the houses and staging; and eventually, the heavy plates and frames for the lantern house and the First Order Fresnel lens system.

The Coast Guard lists the Estevan light as 30.5m (102 ft.) high, and 38.1m (127 ft.) above the water. The diaphone, installed in 1908, was replaced in 1972 with electronic signals, but the old system is still there. The beautiful Fresnel lens was removed long ago and rests in the lanternhouse from Triangle Island on the grounds of the Victoria Coast Guard Agency. Banks of sealed beam lights rotate, giving the flashes characteristic of the station. Early on, Estevan was made a radio beacon station and it remains so today.

An event on June 20, 1942 drew international attention to this remote point on British Columbia's west coast. According to official accounts, Japanese submarine 1-26 surfaced a couple of nautical miles offshore and fired more than twenty shells towards the lighthouse. The motivation remains a mystery. A stray, unexploded shell from the incident was found as late as 1973, when keeper Weeden's wife was out for a walk. Its remote location makes access to the Estevan light difficult.

NORTHWARD *to* PRINCE RUPERT

Langara Island, British Columbia

Triple Island

BC-13

Triple Island, B.C. near Prince Rupert, and Gannet Rock in the Bay of Fundy are the closest Canada has to wave-washed light stations. Both lights are swept by the huge waves of the open ocean, with the added hazard at Triple Island of tsunamis (sometimes misnamed 'tidal waves'). The site was first marked with an automatic gas light in about 1910 but it was never satisfactory. As Prince Rupert grew in maritime importance, lighting of its approaches had to be improved. In 1915, the first detailed surveys were begun for a substantial station. During the first year of construction (1919), the top of one of the Triple Islands was pared off and concrete foundations were poured, anchored deep into the rock. Construction proved difficult, however, and was only possible when rough weather and tides allowed. Supplies were lost in storms and work crews were often terrified when waves washed into their temporary housing.

Over the next couple of years, however, a three-story, bunker-like building rose on the rock. It had living quarters on the top floor, an engine room, the light itself, pumps, and a workshop for on-site repairs. The bottom floor, right on the rock, had the furnace room with coal bins, fuel tanks for the engines, and large rainwater cisterns. The light tower, at one corner of the main building, was an octagonal column flaring out at the top to support the light platform. It was fitted with a Chance Brothers Fresnel lens system of the 3rd Order.

After completion in 1920, this well-constructed station has resisted all of the sea's hungry efforts to wrest it from its tiny island perch. It has withstood stormy seas, earthquakes and tsunamis. The whole station was refurbished and upgraded in 1965, and is automated. It is listed as a white tower 18.9m (63 ft.) tall and 29.6m (99 ft.) above the sea—quite a prosaic description for one of Canada's finest lights, and a true feat in engineering.

Langara Point

At the turn of the century, Prince Rupert grew beyond a simple fishing port and supply centre for northern British Columbia. When it became the western terminus of the Grand Trunk Pacific Railway, a landfall light was needed for the entrance to the Dixon Passage, along with better aids to navigation at the northern end of the Inside Passage. The extreme northwest corner of the Queen Charlotte Islands was an obvious place to build and several sites were surveyed. A location was chosen on North Island, and the island's name was changed back to Langara (an earlier name given by a Spanish admiral). The change was wise, for there are dozens of "North Islands" scattered along Canadian coasts.

Col. Anderson designed a hexagonal tower with joined buttresses at the corners, which flared out to provide a generous platform for the Chance Brothers lantern house and First Order lens. It looks ungainly because the lamphouse is of standard size on a short tower. Construction started in 1911, and its powerful beam first shone over the sea in late 1913.

When I landed here one rainy day, the helicopter crew made a beeline for the house. They knew that Mrs. Redhead, the keeper's wife, would have coffee and her famous muffins waiting. I asked the keeper if he'd take me for a tour right away, because time was short and the weather was growing worse. We walked together down the long, wooden ramp through the dense and wet rain forest, and to the cove where, in calm weather, supplies can be landed. We went up to the tower to see the spotless light, the beautiful prisms of the Fresnel lens system and the wonderful seascape spread out below. Then came a surprise: the tsunami gauge.

As an old geologist, I was particularly interested in the intense seismic activity in the Gulf of Alaska and how tremendous waves, "tsunamis", are generated when earthquakes happen under the sea. Tsunamis pose a special hazard to west-coast lighthouses—throughout the last century, they have smashed station after station, sweeping keepers to their deaths. In a 1946 tsunami, the entire light station at Scotch Cap in the Aleutians simply disappeared along with its five keepers.

Out on the open ocean, tsunamis are scarcely visible, but they have wave lengths as much as 150-300 kms and they travel at 600-750 kms per hour. When they encounter shallow water on shorelines they shorten and become enormously steep walls of raging water, as high as 30m (100 ft.), sweeping everything before them. After Port Alberni on Vancouver Island was flooded in 1964, causing millions of dollars in damage, Canada joined a UNESCO network of tsunami stations in the Pacific. Langara Island light was chosen as an observation site. At regular intervals, the keeper reads the sea level indicator and reports any aberrant behaviour to the network. With signals coming in from all around the northern Pacific, a clear picture emerges, with warnings relayed to countries in the path of the massive waves.

Letter written on door by former keeper.

Lightkeeper Charles Redhead

Epilogue

"...a great commercial nation such as England should not suffer the borders of the great high-road to Canada and her North American possessions to be thus strewed with the property and bodies of her subjects. [Lighthouses]... would be the means of great good."

J.B. Jukes, first Newfoundland
government geologist, 1839

"How far that little candle throws his beams!
So shines a good deed in a naughty world."

Portia in <u>The Merchant of Venice</u>,
Act V, Scene 1; *W. Shakespeare*

Acknowledgments

The writer is especially grateful to the Canadian Coast Guard without whose help this compendium of Canadian lighthouses, scattered along the world's longest coastline, would not have been possible. From officials in Ottawa such as Bill Bertholet, to each of the agencies from St. John's to Victoria, generous help was cheerfully given in transportation, with anecdotes and good company in a shared love and respect for lighthouses and what they have stood for. I am also proud to have met and to acknowledge the help of keepers and their families on stations on the outskirts of major ports, on lonely shores, and on remote islands. My only regret is that so many of them have had to give up their way of life in late years in the face of automation and changing times.

Officials in public archives, notably National Archives of Canada, Provincial Archives of Newfoundland, and Victoria, and museums have been most helpful, as have been many staff members of Historic Sites (Canada). The research of E.F. Bush, published by that department, is essential for any modern lighthouse scholar in this country.

A special word of thanks and encouragement to people working to preserve our lights, such as the Friends of the Yarmouth Light (N.S.) and the Southwest Development Association (Nfld.) who did not hesitate to share their experiences and resources with me. My thanks go to the editors and staff of my publishers, Lynx Images, Inc., for their continued assistance through the long process of preparing a book from a manuscript and a collection of photographs.

An interest in lighthouses spanning the period between my first visit in 1935 to the Partridge Island station (Saint John, N.B.) and keeper Lauder and the borrowing of photographs from the Victoria agency in early 1999 must invariably involve generous help from hundreds of people. I beg forgiveness for not listing them all but hope that they will understand and accept my heartfelt thanks. Perhaps they will see their favourite lights in this book and remember.

References and Selected Readings

Adams, W.H.D. *Lighthouses and Lightships*. London: T. Nelson and Son, 1871.

Bush, E.F. *The Canadian Lighthouse*. Canadian Historic Sites: Occasional Papers in Archaeology and History, No. 9, pp. 5-110. Ottawa, 1975.

Canadian Coast Guard. Occasional Pamphlets such as "East Point, B.C." (Saturna) and "Active Pass, B.C.". Undated, probably early 1990s.

Canadian Coast Guard. Marine Navigation Services. *List of Lights, Buoys and Fog Signals*. Ottawa: Fisheries and Oceans Canada.
_____.Atlantic Coast, 1987 and 1998.
_____.Inland Waters, 1981.
_____.Newfoundland, 1981 and 1998.
_____.Pacific Coast, 1981.

Gibbs, J.A. *Lighthouses of the Pacific*. West Chester: Schiffer Publishing Co., 1986.

Graham, D. *Keepers of the Light: A History of British Columbia's Lighthouses and Their Keepers*. Madeira Park: Harbour Publishing Ltd., 1987.

Gutsche, A., Chisholm, B., and Floren, R. *Alone in the Night*. Toronto: Lynx Images Inc., 1996.

Holland, F.R. *Lighthouses*. New York: Friedman/Fairfax Publishers, 1995.

Jukes, J.B. *Excursions In and About Newfoundland During the Years 1839 and 1840*, vol. 1. London: John Murray, 1842.

Lafrenière, N. *Lightkeeping on the St. Lawrence*. Toronto: Dundern Press, 1996.

Molloy, D.J. *The First Landfall: Historic Lighthouses of Newfoundland and Labrador*. St. John's: Breakwater, 1994.

Richardson, E.M. *We Keep a Light*. Toronto: Ryerson Press, 1945.

Smallwood, Joseph R., editor in chief and Pitt, R.D.W., managing editor. *Encyclopedia of Newfoundland*. St John's: Newfoundland Book Publishers, 1981-1994.

Stephens, D.E. *Lighthouses of Nova Scotia*. Hantsport: Lancelot Press, 1973.

Stephens, D. and Randles, S. *Discover Nova Scotia Lighthouses*. Halifax: Nimbus Publishing, 1998.

Talbot, F.A. *Lightships and Lighthouses*. London: William Heinemann, 1913.

Thurston, H and Barrett, W. *Against Darkness and Storm, Lighthouses of the Northeast*. Halifax: Nimbus, 1993.

Whitney, D. *The Lighthouse*. Toronto: McClelland and Stewart, 1975.

Zinck, J. *Shipwrecks of Nova Scotia*. Vol. 2. Hantsport: Lancelot Press, 1977.

Photo Credits

All photographs are by the author except those from the following sources:

Adams, W.D.: p. 18 bottom left and right

Canadian Coast Guard (Victoria - Mike Mitchell): Apologia right, 211, 214 lower

Chance Bros. Catalogue: p. 18, upper right

Illustrated London News: Preface

Maritime Museum of the Great Lakes at Kingston: 16, 19 top

National Archives of Canada: 3, 43, 69 upper left, 77, 92, 178

National Library of Canada: 3, 62 upper left

Southwest Coast Development Association (Nfld.): 9 upper right, 62 lower left

Talbot, F.A.: 179 upper left corner, 197

David McCurdy Baird

Born in Fredericton, New Brunswick, David Baird spent five years of his early childhood in China with his missionary parents. Returning to Canada, he lived in Canning, N.S., and Saint John, N.B., before attending the University of New Brunswick. He has a Masters degree in Science from the University of Rochester, and a Doctorate from McGill University.

Dr. Baird has a well-established background in public education with numerous popular science books and papers, TV programs and public lectures. During his distinguished career, he was Founding Director of the National Museum of Science and Technology in Ottawa, and went on to hold positions at the Tyrrell Museum of Palaeontology and the Rideau Canal Museum. During 1988-89, he gave an address in several Canadian cities for the Royal Canadian Geographical Society, entitled, "Lighthouses: The Vanishing Sentinels." Dr. Baird was made an Officer, Order of Canada in 1986 for his outstanding contributions to natural sciences, education and museums. Aside from his formal professional activities, he has had a lifetime fascination with lighthouses, and has visited and photographed hundreds of them in Canada and in scores of other countries.

ABOUT LYNX IMAGES

Lynx Images is a unique book publishing and film production company that specializes in exploring and documenting vanishing pieces of Canadian history. The company's Great Lakes focus has generated several best-selling books and films:

* Mysterious Islands: Forgotten Tales of the Great Lakes
* Superior: Under the Shadow of the Gods
* Enchanted Summers: The Grand Hotels of Muskoka
* Ghosts of the Bay: The Forgotten History of Georgian Bay
* Alone in the Night: Lighthouses of Georgian Bay, Manitoulin Island and the North Channel
* The North Channel and St. Mary's River: A Guide to the History

Also from Lynx Images

ALONE IN THE NIGHT:
Lighthouses of Georgian Bay, Manitoulin Island and the North Channel
Book and Video

Lighthouses capture the imagination with their fascinating stories and forgotten memories. Alone in the Night is a compelling journey to the lighthouses of Georgian Bay, Manitoulin Island, and the North Channel. It traces the evolution of lightkeeping, revealing the heroic and scandalous, gritty and routine aspects of this remarkable chapter of Canada's marine heritage.

In the book, discover the over 50 lighthouse sites through stories, 400 photographs, and maps. The film's stunning cinematography, archival footage and photographs return viewers to a time when the Great Lakes were the lifeblood of the country.

FOR A CATALOGUE OR TO ORDER, CONTACT:

Lynx Images Inc.
P.O. Box 5961, Stn. A
Toronto, Ontario M5W 1P4

www. lynximages.com

ISBN 0-9698427-4-0 Book/Video
ISBN 0-9698427-5-9 Video
ISBN 0-9698427-6-7 Book

Index